Cambridge Elements

Elements on Women in the History of Philosophy
edited by
Jacqueline Broad
Monash University

HARRIET JACOBS

Alan. M. S. J. Coffee
King's College London

Shaftesbury Road, Cambridge CB2 8EA, United Kingdom

One Liberty Plaza, 20th Floor, New York, NY 10006, USA

477 Williamstown Road, Port Melbourne, VIC 3207, Australia

314–321, 3rd Floor, Plot 3, Splendor Forum, Jasola District Centre, New Delhi – 110025, India

103 Penang Road, #05-06/07, Visioncrest Commercial, Singapore 238467

Cambridge University Press is part of Cambridge University Press & Assessment, a department of the University of Cambridge.

We share the University's mission to contribute to society through the pursuit of education, learning and research at the highest international levels of excellence.

www.cambridge.org
Information on this title: www.cambridge.org/9781009318426

DOI: 10.1017/9781009318457

© Alan M. S. J. Coffee 2025

This publication is in copyright. Subject to statutory exception and to the provisions of relevant collective licensing agreements, no reproduction of any part may take place without the written permission of Cambridge University Press & Assessment.

When citing this work, please include a reference to the DOI 10.1017/9781009318457

First published 2025

A catalogue record for this publication is available from the British Library

ISBN 978-1-009-61939-4 Hardback
ISBN 978-1-009-31842-6 Paperback
ISSN 2634-4645 (online)
ISSN 2634-4637 (print)

Cambridge University Press & Assessment has no responsibility for the persistence or accuracy of URLs for external or third-party internet websites referred to in this publication and does not guarantee that any content on such websites is, or will remain, accurate or appropriate.

For EU product safety concerns, contact us at Calle de José Abascal, 56, 1°, 28003 Madrid, Spain, or email eugpsr@cambridge.org

Harriet Jacobs

Elements on Women in the History of Philosophy

DOI: 10.1017/9781009318457
First published online: October 2025

Alan. M. S. J. Coffee
King's College London
Author for correspondence: Alan. M. S. J. Coffee, alan.coffee@kcl.ac.uk

Abstract: Long celebrated for her heroic feat of endurance in escaping slavery and subsequent activism, Harriet Jacobs was also an astute political thinker. Her book, *Incidents in the Life of a Slave Girl*, is a remarkable philosophical text. It is one of the most insightful reflections, both on the nature of life as a slave, and on the relationships amongst slaves and between enslaved and free people. The author places Jacobs in the republican tradition of political thought. Bringing Jacobs into dialogue with Frederick Douglass, the author argues that Jacobs's emphasis on sexual abuse and the importance of slave relationships offers us a basis for a feminist republicanism. Jacobs also emphasises the structural nature of slavery, reinforced by propaganda and social prejudices. These implicate not just slaveholders but also the free population in slavery's wrongs.

Keywords: Harriet Jacobs, slavery, Republicanism, feminism, freedom

© Alan. M. S. J. Coffee 2025

ISBNs: 9781009619394 (HB), 9781009318426 (PB), 9781009318457 (OC)
ISSNs: 2634-4645 (online), 2634-4637 (print)

Contents

1 Introduction — 1

2 Freedom as Independence — 13

3 Agency, Dignity and Virtue — 24

4 Feminist Republicanism — 38

5 Structural Domination — 52

6 Final Reflections — 65

Cast of Characters — 68

List of Abbreviations — 70

References — 71

1 Introduction

Harriet Jacobs (1813–1897) was an American abolitionist and educator. She is remembered mainly for her autobiography, *Incidents in the Life of a Slave Girl* (1861), in which she recounts her life as a slave, the events that led to her dramatic escape, and subsequent experiences as a fugitive in the supposedly free northern states. Written under a pseudonym, this was Jacobs's only book. It has, nevertheless, become a classic – not just as a slave narrative but as a literary gem in its own right. For a short book, *Incidents* is a towering personal achievement, and a unique contribution to American history. Its evocative portrayal of the relationships both amongst slaves and between slaveholders and their human property makes *Incidents* a philosophically rich text that rewards close and sustained study.

I approach Jacobs's work as a political philosopher. Jacobs herself almost certainly did not think of herself in this way, of course. Aside from being taught the basics of reading and writing from her first mistress, she received no education and was entirely self-taught. She did not write a formal treatise or engage with the writings of other philosophers but instead told her personal story in a style that often resembles that of a romantic novel. In her preface to *Incidents*, however, Jacobs makes her political aims clear. 'I do earnestly desire', she says, 'to arouse the women of the North to a realizing sense of the condition of two millions of women at the South, still in bondage, suffering what I suffered, and most of them far worse', adding that she hopes that this will 'convince the people of the Free States what Slavery really is' (*Incidents*, 5). To these aims, her novelistic autobiographical style seems more suited than a simple testimony or logical diagnosis: 'only by experience', she argues, 'can any one realize how deep, and dark, and foul is that pit of abominations'.

Although Jacobs does not write as a philosopher, this does not mean that her work lacks an ideological framework or structure. She did not formulate her ideas in a vacuum but situated herself in the abolitionist intellectual and political debates of the nineteenth century. Although *Incidents* is a memoir, it is written as a slave narrative, which is a genre with a distinctive literary form – even if she does push the boundaries of expectation within it (Ernest 2014). Slave narratives, of course, did not merely depict slavery, they were written to challenge and undermine the institution. In the United States, authors often drew on the conceptual legacy of the American Revolution in making their arguments. Jacobs was no exception. In particular, I shall place her thought in what is now referred to as the republican political tradition centred around a specific conception of freedom, understood as independence. There are several advantages in interpreting Jacobs's work using this framework. First, her use of terms and ideals associated with this tradition is clear. Furthermore, several other African American writers of the period also make use of this conceptual framework – including David Walker, Maria Stewart, Samuel Ringgold Ward and, most significantly for our purposes, Frederick Douglass – and wrote within the same tradition (Coffee 2020, 2024, Gooding-Williams 2011, Rogers 2023). This not only serves as a useful reference point in understanding Jacobs's own ideas but also allows us to bring her work into dialogue with other abolitionists, deepening our understanding of the development of black activist political thought in the nineteenth century. Thirdly, I argue that Jacobs offers valuable innovations on the basic republican model that should interest feminist republicans.

In analysing Jacobs's work through a republican lens, I do not mean to restrict the scope of her thought or to privilege this particular vantage point. Although she has not yet been the subject of sustained scholarship by political philosophers, a considerable body of work exists on *Incidents*, mostly by literary theorists, feminists and scholars of African American studies. The Second Norton Critical Edition of *Incidents* that I use for my references in this Element includes several excellent essays giving context and analysis, drawing comparisons with other narrative texts such as those by Olaudah Equiano, Sojourner Truth and Frederick Douglass and examining themes of voice, class, race, gender, domesticity and motherhood, sexual assault, amongst others. A number of these essays had earlier been anthologised in a volume on *Harriet Jacobs and Incidents: New Critical Essays* (Garfield and Zafar 1996). Also included is Jean Yellin's landmark article 'Written by Herself: Harriet Jacobs' Slave Narrative' (1981) which settled all speculation about Jacobs's authorship of *Incidents*. Yellin followed this with a comprehensive biography, *Harriet Jacobs: A Life* (2004). Jacobs's writing has also formed part of broader analyses of the slavery legacy, such as Hortense Spillers's 'Mama's Baby, Papa's Maybe' or Saidiya Hartman's *Scenes of Subjection* which look at black women's sexual vulnerability in part through the account given in *Incidents* (Spillers 1987, Hartman 1997). Nick Bromell brings aspects of Jacobs's thought into dialogue with contemporary political discourse, first, in his book *The Time Is Always Now*, and more fully in 'Harriet Jacobs: Prisoner of Hope' in which he analyses what he sees as her scepticism of 'the idea of futurity' (2013, 2021).

Impressive and valuable as these sources are, however, with the exception of Yellin, I make very little reference to them in what follows. Since my focus is on political philosophy, my concern will be with the tools, concepts and questions that arise from that discipline. Most of my attention will be on Jacobs's texts rather than analysing the secondary literature. A further article that deserves mention at this point is Desmond Jagmohan's 'Peculiar Property: Harriet Jacobs on the Nature of Slavery' (2022). This is an excellent paper that challenges the emphasis that I place on republicanism as an analytical tool in both understanding slavery in general and Jacobs's philosophy in particular. Since I do not want to get ahead of my own arguments in this introduction, I respond to Jagmohan's position in this note.[1]

---

[1] Jagmohan (2022) distinguishes between *de facto* and *de jure* accounts of slavery, arguing that neo-republican accounts adopt the former, while Jacobs works within the latter. According to Jagmohan, Jacobs regards the essence of slavery to be that it makes property out of human beings. The absolute nature of that property relationship – whereby holders are authorised to use, dispose of, and even to waste or destroy their property at their discretion – is said to account for the unique evil of slavery. Jagmohan himself does not reject the republican account, and accepts that it has some advantages in expressing certain salient aspects such as the continuities in black oppression between the pre- and postbellum periods. Republicanism, however, is said not to be able to capture all slavery's harms. Jagmohan argues that republicans are committed to treating the aspect of property holding in people as simply a particularly intense form of domination, which is the republican's central disvalue, rather than as a distinct harm in itself.

Although I agree with much of the substance of Jagmohan's analysis, I nevertheless retain the republican framework. My reason is partly historical and contextual – given the republican ideals prevalent in abolitionist and broader political discourse at that time – and partly textual, based on my reading of Jacobs's work. Even if one does not wish to read Jacobs as a republican herself, analysing her work through a republican lens would remain a valuable exercise for contemporary republican theorists. My own model of republicanism, however, differs from the kind Jagmohan critiques. Rather than an account of interpersonal, *de facto*, domination, I adopt a structural approach in which domination is both interpersonal and structural, thereby accommodating the institutional authority and wider social complicity that a *de jure* account entails (Coffee 2024).

I am sympathetic to Jagmohan's wish to avoid placing slavery at the extreme end of a continuum of types of domination. On my understanding, institutionalised chattel slavery is a distinctive (and not merely more intense) form of domination. That slavery as property *is* a form of arbitrary controlling power is, I believe, undeniable. Accordingly, slavery *must* fall within the scope of domination. However, not all forms of arbitrary power are to be understood or treated in the same way (I elaborate on this in note 7). For example, elsewhere, I distinguish between cultural power, on the one hand, and legal power, on the other, arguing that each must be understood and addressed on its own terms (2014, 2024). Similarly, chattel slavery's institutional establishment and the nature of making persons into property are unique features requiring their own analysis, albeit within the concept of domination.

Finally, while the nature of servitude as property is certainly important to Jacobs's thinking, I argue that this alone does not account for the specific harms that women face as sexualised objects. She also emphasises the role of patriarchy, for example. She notes that women slaveholders are far less likely to abuse their slaves than men (*Incidents*, 70), and that slaveholders' wives were often powerless to intervene in the practice of abuse that was often also abhorrent to them.

1.1 The Life of a Slave Girl

Harriet Jacobs was born in 1813 in the small town of Edenton in North Carolina, the daughter of two slaves and so a slave herself. This simple statement, though factual, belies the complicated story of sexual abuse, emancipation, kidnap and re-enslavement, and broken promises that beset the family over five generations, and the spirit of independence, dignity and self-assertion that they cultivated and maintained. Nor does it reflect close blood relationships between the families of slaves and the families of slaveholders.

At the age of twelve, Jacobs was bequeathed to the five-year-old Mary Matilda Norcom, becoming the de facto property of the girl's father, Dr James Norcom. From the time that she entered the Norcom's house, she began to understand the 'guilty practices' that were part of every female slave's reality but which could never be spoken about (*Incidents*, 28). By the time she was fifteen, Norcom – some thirty-five years her senior – had taken a sexual interest in her. However, although abuse was ubiquitous within the slaveholding community, there is no suggestion from Jacobs that he raped or molested her (although he did physically strike and threaten her). Indeed, Jacobs's resistance to, and eventual victory over, her tormentor forms an important part of her story, and the analysis we shall give. This said, for all her personal heroism, she is emphatic that she was fortunate. Reflecting on the horrors of the plantations from which she had been spared, she exclaims, 'God pity the woman who is compelled to lead such a life!' (98).

When Norcom forbade Jacobs from entering into a relationship with a free black man – a carpenter like her father – he made plans to install her in a secluded house four miles from town, out of view from prying eyes. She sought refuge through the attentions of a neighbouring slaveholder and future congressman, Samuel Treadwell Sawyer, with whom she had two children, Joseph and Louisa Matilda. Both would become Norcom's property and be used as weapons against her. Faced with the prospect of being transferred to a plantation where her children would be 'broke in', Jacobs absconds. She then contrives through a ruse to have her children sold to Sawyer, a comparatively safer prospect than the vindictive Norcom, although Jacobs had learned never to trust a slaveholder. Despite promising to free the children – his own children – Sawyer never did. Unwilling to lose sight of her children until they were safely out of slavery, Jacobs remained hidden in a tiny crawl space above the porch-like shelter attached to her grandmother's house. Described as a garret in the book, its floor measured only three metres by two, and was only one metre at its highest point, though it tapered with the slope of the roof, being triangular in its cross section. There was barely space to turn, let alone stand, and the space lacked insulation, ventilation, light or damp-proofing. There were also rats.

Finding a discarded gimlet, Jacobs bored an inch-wide peephole through which she could watch her children play and listen to snatches of gossip. She remained hidden in this space for seven years, not even emerging for exercise for the first five. Jacobs wrote post-dated letters to her grandmother and to Norcom which were smuggled north and mailed home, as if she were living in New York. Only once Louisa Matilda had been sent to Sawyer's relatives in Brooklyn – ostensibly to receive an education, although this was, again, a hollow promise – and with the reasonable expectation that Joseph would soon travel north with her uncle Mark Ramsey, did Jacobs herself make the perilous journey to a free state.

The notion of a 'free state' proved to be a misnomer. The United States was a single country in which the interests of slaveholding states still held sway. Jacobs was not a citizen with rights and privileges. Instead, she was a fugitive living in the margins of society. Even before the passing of the infamous Fugitive Slave Law of 1850 – which required officials in all states to participate in the recapture of slaves and punished anyone giving assistance to a fugitive – Jacobs was constantly on the lookout for traps set by her pursuers. She took her ongoing battle with the Norcoms in her stride. More upsetting to her personally was the realisation that black people had a second-class status, being subject to rigid segregation laws and public hostility. At least the racial hierarchy in the south was overt, Jacobs lamented. Whereas northern inhabitants prided themselves on their enlightened views about human freedom and dignity on the surface, she found everywhere 'the same manifestations of that cruel prejudice, which so discourages the feelings, and represses the energies of the colored people' (146).

Jacobs found work as a nursemaid to the daughter of an Englishwoman, Mary Stace Willis. She was married to the popular author and poet, Nathaniel Parker Willis. Though Jacobs regarded Nathaniel as being proslavery (*Papers* 191), Mary was a kind and generous employer and friend, helping Jacobs relocate to Boston when the Norcoms were on her trail.[2]

---

[2] Lydia Maria Child notes that, Willis's *Home Journal*, 'is not *violently* pro-slavery, but it is very *insidiously* and *systematically* so', adding that the journal was one of three singled out by Jefferson Davis's organs as 'the only Northern papers that the South could securely *trust*' (*Papers*, 343, her emphasis).

When Mary sadly died in childbirth, Nathaniel took Jacobs as his daughter's nanny with him on a trip to England to visit the bereaved relatives. He later married Cornelia Grinnell, an ardently anti-slavery native of New Bedford, MA. With the passing of the Fugitive Slave Act, the dangers facing Jacobs and her children rose dramatically. Although Jacobs vehemently objected to the idea that her freedom could be bought – 'I could not possibly regard myself as a piece of property' (154) – Cornelia, grasping the gravity of the situation, secretly arranged to purchase the freedom of not only Jacobs but also her children for $300.

Jacobs was emotionally torn. On the one hand, that she had been traded as a chattel was a bitter pill – '"The bill of sale!" Those words struck me like a blow. So I was sold at last! A human being sold in the free city of New York!' (*Incidents*, 164, see *Papers*, 180–1). On the other hand, she was moved by the love shown by her friend, a word that struck a chord – 'God had raised me up a friend among strangers, who had bestowed on me the precious, long-desired boon. Friend! It is a common word, often lightly used. Like other good and beautiful things, it may be tarnished by careless handling; but when I speak of Mrs. Bruce as my friend, the word is sacred' (*Incidents* 165). Jacobs recalled in the final pages of her book, how in the opening pages her father and grandmother had worked hard to save the money to buy their family's freedom. In fact, the sum of $300 may have been especially poignant since it was the same sum that her grandmother had been swindled out of by her mistress right at the start of her story, money that had been carefully saved to buy her children's freedom. Jacobs fondly imagined, 'how that faithful, loving old heart would leap for joy, if she could look on me and my children now that we were free!'

1.2 Writing

After Mary Stace Willis's death, Jacobs relocated for a time to Rochester, New York. Situated on the shore of Lake Ontario, across from free Canada, Rochester had become an influential centre for abolitionists. There, she ran an anti-slavery reading room with her brother, John Swanson Jacobs, noting that there was not sufficient local interest for the venture to be viable (156). When the Fugitive Slave Act came into force, John – himself a runaway – left Rochester, trying his luck as a gold prospector first in California and then Australia. Harriet wished that she could have gone with him, but felt a lasting burden of debt to Cornelia Willis for having purchased her, another serious drawback to the commodification of her body and soul (*Papers*, 185–6). Though John shared his sister's revulsion at being purchased himself, he accepted a promise made by Cornelia Willis to ensure that Harriet was out of the reach of the slave hunters (*Papers*, 147–8).

John's master had been Sawyer – the father to Harriet's children – whom he deserted in New York while Harriet was in hiding. Not having children to factor in to his calculations, John had been able to bide his time – ingratiating himself with Sawyer to become 'a most faithful servant, and ... valued friend' – until an opportune moment presented itself (*Incidents*, 112). John did not like the duplicity which circumstances forced upon him – feeling it to be beneath the dignity of a self-respecting human being – but accepted that he owed no obligation to slaveholders under the unjust institution they upheld. Sawyer had trusted him and had wanted a good life for him ('if there can be any life for a slave', John adds, *Despots*, 50). He only took from Sawyer what he felt was necessary – which included his pistols for protection, indicating the life and death nature of what was at stake.[3] As a man, John wished Sawyer no ill. 'The lawyer', he wrote of Sawyer, 'I have a quite friendly feeling for, and would be pleased to meet him as a countryman and a brother, but not as a master' (50). Sorry not to have bid him farewell in person, he left a short note which he signed, 'No longer yours, John S Jacob' (49, original spelling).

John wrote his own autobiographical narrative, two versions of which are in existence. The original, provocatively entitled *The United States Governed by Six Hundred Thousand Despots: A True Story of Slavery*, was published in an Australian newspaper in 1855. This version was lost until it was unearthed by Jonathan Schroeder in 2016, and republished in 2024. Publication in Australia, Schroeder notes, had given John licence to speak out in the fieriest of terms against slavery. He had then intended to have the manuscript published in London, depositing the papers with a weekly magazine while he went out to sea on a whaling voyage. He returned the following year to find his work edited, sanitised, cut in half and given the more anodyne title, *A True Tale of Slavery*. The original version had been divided into eleven sections, with the final three critiquing the United States laws and constitution. The bowdlerised version entirely omitted these, leaving John somewhat in his sister's literary shadow. With the availability of *Despots*, his witness to and perspectives on the evils of slavery and the nation that permitted it may yet be restored.

---

[3] John told Cornelia Willis that he was prepared to use his pistols to protect Harriet from 'the fleshmongers' (*Despots*, 55).

In Rochester, Harriet mixed with a powerful subset of abolitionist activists, including Frederick Douglass and Amy Post, the woman who would encourage and support her in publishing *Incidents*. Understandably, writing did not come easily to Jacobs. For one thing, she had had no education other than some basic literacy from her well-meaning first mistress (a 'privilege, which so rarely falls to the lot of a slave', *Incidents*, 12). Her job in Rochester would have given her ample access to suitable reading materials, as well as the opportunity to meet, listen to and discuss with leading activist figures. But none of this could have adequately prepared her for the subtly layered and finely crafted work that she ultimately produced – a testament to a staggering intellectual ability. Gifted as she may have been, Jacobs also needed the opportunity to hone and sharpen her writing skills. This she did in part through writing (anonymously) to the newspapers. In June 1853, her first letter was published in the *New York Daily Tribune*. In the letter, she highlighted the sexual abuse that was rife in the plantations, observing that 'a slaveholder seldom takes a white mistress, for she is an expensive commodity, not as submissive as he would like to have her, but more apt to be tyrannical; and when his passion seeks another object, he must leave her in quiet possession of all the gewgaws that she has sold herself for' (*Papers*, 200. We discuss this letter and its context in §§5.2–5.3).

A second barrier to writing was her sense of shame about her story. Although she had resisted Norcom, she felt sullied by him, and by succumbing to Sawyer, she believed that she had let herself and her family down. She was also indignant at the judgements of others. When, for example, a reverend praises her candidness but warns that others may treat her more scornfully, she writes, 'that word contempt burned me like coals of fire' (*Incidents* 135). It took considerable courage on Jacobs's part to tell the truth about Sawyer, even to her own daughter. Only after they had been living in Boston for two years together could she summon the nerve, and only then as Louisa was departing for boarding school. Jacobs felt similarly with Amy Post, to whom she wrote, 'you know a woman can whisper her cruel wrongs in the ear of a dear friend much easier than she can record them for the world to read' (168).

Thirdly, Jacobs simply had to find time to write. The book was completed while working as a nursemaid for the Willises in their country home on the Hudson river, Idlewild. Their home was established as a writing retreat. Jacobs, however, kept the project to herself, unable to endure the patronising 'criticism and ridicule of Educated people'. She worked on the manuscript only after her chores were done, and even then, in secret. A friend, she recalls, 'saw from my daily duties that a single page was hard for me to find much time to write as yet I have not written a single page by daylight', adding that 'with the care of the little baby and the big Babies and at the household calls I have but a little time to think or write', *Incidents*, 198, *Papers*, 213).[4]

Yet another hurdle almost proved to be decisive, that of finding a publisher. This is problem enough for any aspiring writer, but for a slave – a female slave, to boot – it was imperative that the book be endorsed, specifically by someone white. Jacobs was adamant that Nathaniel Willis could not be approached – he 'would tell me it was very wrong and that I was trying to do harm' (*Papers*, 191).[5] Harriet Beecher Stowe – whose *Uncle Tom's Cabin* had just been published – was asked, but she bluntly declined. Instead, Stowe offered only to include it in her *A Key to Uncle Tom's Cabin*, which compiled documented true stories of slavery to support the authenticity of the earlier novel. In the end, Lydia Maria Child agreed to endorse *Incidents*, supplying an introduction and postscript. This much achieved, the next challenge was to find a publisher. A visit to England in 1858 proved unsuccessful. The search weighed heavily on Jacobs's spirits. In 1860, she wrote to Post, 'when I returned home from Europe, I said that I would not mention my M S. to my friends again until I had done something with it – little dreaming of the time that might elapse – but as time wore on difficulties seemed to thicken and I became discouraged. I felt that I had cut myself off from my friends' (*Papers*, 282). Eventually, a publisher was found, only for it to go bust. Jacobs then bought the plates and arranged for the book to be printed and bound herself (Yellin 2004, 143). Shortly afterwards, the book was published in England under the title *The Deeper Wrong; or, Incidents in the Life of a Slave Girl.*

1.3 Anonymity, Recognition, Obscurity

Incidents was published under a pseudonym as *Linda, or Incidents in the Life of a Slave Girl, Written by Herself*. Jacobs adopted the name Linda Brent, and all other names were changed. I use the real names of those I discuss in this Element since I not only draw on *Incidents* but on Jacobs's letters and family papers, as well as on her brother's narrative which was not pseudonymised. There were several reasons why *Incidents* was published

---

[4] In another letter, Jacobs wrote, 'I have been interrupted and called away so often – that I hardly know what I have written' (*Incidents* 201).

[5] Child notes that Willis 'often entertains many Southerners at Idlewild, and is a favorite with them; for that reason the author of "Linda" did not ask <u>him</u> to help her about her M S. though he has always been friendly to her, and would have more influence than I have' (*Papers*, 343, her emphasis).

anonymously. Child outlines some of the considerations in a letter to the poet and activist, John Greenleaf Whittier, indicating that Jacobs was concerned about possible embarrassment to, and reprisals against, her family and allies in the South, as well as to Cornelia Willis who would not welcome the public attention (*Papers*, 343).

A more personal factor driving her anonymity was the nature of the material itself. As we noted earlier, the book's content contained events that Jacobs found difficult even to whisper to a friend. Though written in understated language by today's standards – and even Jacobs accepts that 'there are somethings that I might have made plainer' – the book was recognised as breaking new ground in its subject matter at the time (236, original spelling). The nineteenth-century reviewer Amelia Chesson described *Incidents* as 'the first personal narrative in which one of that sex upon whom chattel servitude falls with the deepest and darkest shadow has ever described her own bitter experience', adding that 'there is no wrong which woman is made to suffer that happier women should shrink from knowing', and that Jacobs has given us 'an insight into the precise nature of the wrongs which are inseparable from slavery in its outwardly most inoffensive and harmless guise' (366). This was just the message that Jacobs wanted to convey. In more modern terms, sexual abuse in all its manifestations was not just widespread or pervasive, it was integral to the institution of slavery itself. As we shall see, although it was the slave women who suffered most directly, no one in a slaveholding nation emerged unscathed by its moral degradation. With this in mind, Jacobs makes this pledge: 'I have left nothing out but what I thought – the world might believe that a Slave woman was too willing to pour out – that she might gain their sympathies …. I have placed myself before you to be judged as a woman …. Whether I deserve your pity or contempt' (236–7).

Groundbreaking as *Incidents* was, it was not the only book published that year to feature a real-life female slave candidly speaking about domestic and sexual abuse. Louisa Picquet's narrative, *Louisa Picquet, the Octoroon, or, Inside Views of Southern Domestic Life*, was, perhaps, even more direct, even if it still relies on innuendo and nuance to make its points. About a quarter of the length of *Incidents*, Picquet's was a very different publication. Rather than having been written alone and in secret, *Octaroon* was a collaboration between Picquet and the abolitionist minister Hiram Mattison, whose questions prompted and shaped the narrative. Furthermore, while Jacobs emphasises the importance of her message, and downplays the financial motive – giving as an additional reason for anonymity the desire not to be seen as indolent and simply writing for the money – Picquet is explicit that she will use the proceeds from the book's sales to buy her mother's freedom, something she was in fact able to do. Though the circumstances shaping Picquet's telling are understandable, they inevitably have a distorting effect on the final product. As a meticulously written, sustained and serious treatment from an authentic voice, *Incidents* stands alone as an analysis of slavery from a woman's perspective, and in very select company as slave literature of any kind.

Although Jacobs initially shrank from identifying herself as Linda, the truth soon became known in literary and abolitionist circles. This earned her a good deal of respect amongst activists, which would be helpful in the next phase of her life as an aid worker and educator during the Civil War. However, as the political debates and public reading habits changed during the late nineteenth century, and into the twentieth, Jacobs's attribution was forgotten. By the 1960s, although Jacobs's authorship was sometimes suggested, the dominant view had come to be that *Incidents* was in fact written by Child herself, with the character Linda having been invented as a literary device.[6] While it is a great testament to Jacobs's skill as a writer, that her book contains the layers, subtleties, structure and compelling narrative of a novel, it meant that her name was effectively erased from history for around a century. It was not until Yellin's definitive documentary account in 1981 that the case was put beyond any doubt that it was Jacobs's own work.

1.4 Activism

Incidents was published in January 1861, just months before the outbreak of the Civil War. Rather than taking the path of public speaking, as her brother had initially done before the Fugitive Slave Act, Jacobs turned her attention to more practical forms of service. She went to Washington, D.C. and Alexandria, Virginia with her daughter to provide relief for the large stream of black refugees crossing into Union controlled territory, known officially and euphemistically as 'contrabands' – confiscated property of traitorous, hostile owners. At the request of the abolitionist, William Lloyd Garrison, Jacobs documented the cramped, squalid, unsanitary conditions of the refugee camps in a report to the *Liberator* magazine (*Papers*, 400–15). It was not only the physical condition of the evacuees and migrants that disturbed Jacobs, however. As so often, she

---

[6] Joanne Braxton (1986) notes that Marion Starling had argued for Jacobs as the author of *Incidents* in 1947. John Blassingame, by contrast, took the view that the book should be attributed to Child (1972).

was appalled by the prejudice and callous disregard displayed by the white population, both amongst the aid workers themselves and in the largely pro-confederate (or 'secesh') local population.

Throughout her letters, Jacobs emphasises and reiterates the humanity, the dignity, the virtue, the willingness to work hard and to learn, and the good faith displayed by the refugees. Responding to the false allegations that 'lying, thieving and licentiousness' was rife amongst the freedmen, Jacobs again writes in the *Liberator*, 'O, when will the white man learn to know the hearts of my abused and suffering people!' (*Papers*, 472, 470). In the same report, she draws attention to the attitude of the black men who want to join the fight for their own freedom, repeating the complaint she hears, 'the white men of the North have helped us thus far, and we want to help them. We would like to fight for them, if only they would treat us like men' (*Papers*, 469).

Of all her projects, education seems closest to Jacobs's heart. In 1864, she established the Jacobs Free School along with her daughter, to serve the local freedmen community in Alexandria. Jacobs considered it imperative that the school's teachers should be black, as did the community itself ('the freedmen had built the school-house for her children, and were Trustees of the school' and it was their 'decision that the colored teachers should have charge of the school', *Papers*, 559). She argued that this was a psychologically significant principle, since it would help nurture a spirit of independence – already present but in need of opportunities to build on it – amongst the freed population. Those 'born and bred in slavery, had always been so accustomed to look upon the white race as their natural superior and masters, that we had some doubts whether they could easily throw off the habit'. She need not have worried, for 'even their brief possession of freedom had begun to inspire them with respect for their race'.

With the end of the Civil War, the Jacobs relocated in 1865 to Savannah, Georgia, representing the New York Yearly Meeting of Friends and the New England Freedmen's Aid Society, opening a free school for the local freedmen (*Papers*, 625). The political climate, however, was changing rapidly, and growing increasingly hostile towards the black population. Harriet warns Child in a letter not to 'believe the stories so often repeated that negroes are not willing to work' (*Papers*, 663) and lists some of the unjust working practices. In a separate letter, she records how freedmen 'must work under their former overseers. They cannot own a horse, cow, pig, or poultry, nor keep a boat; and they cannot leave the plantation without permission' (657). The legal system was also stacked against them, with Louisa writing that 'the chains have fallen off from them, but justice has not yet found an echo in the hearts of their old oppressors …. Arrests are frequently made, and fines and punishments inflicted without any proof of guilt. For the slightest offence a colored man is sentenced for thirty days, or six months, to the chain gang' (668).

2 Freedom as Independence

In placing Jacobs in a republican context, I have in mind a very specific sense. As I use the term, 'republican' refers only to the use of its characteristic understanding of freedom as independence nestled within a suite of related values. I do not intend to label Jacobs herself as a 'republican thinker' – although the label would likely make sense, given the intellectual and political company she kept within abolitionist circles – since she does not address the broader questions – such as institutional design or the nature of legitimate authority through accountability to the people – that we might think of as characteristic of the republican tradition. What she does, however, is draw on and work within a clearly republican structure, both challenging and reworking some of its prevailing assumptions concerning the agency and complex inner lives of the oppressed, particularly with respect to the importance of personal and family relationships. She also forces us to rethink masculine biases by presenting a feminist perspective that includes an acknowledgement of the ubiquity and significance of sexual abuse against women as a form of arbitrary power that must be addressed by republicans.

Independence was the dominant conception of freedom in Anglophone moral and political philosophy throughout the seventeenth and eighteenth centuries and had a prominent place in the rhetoric and discourse of the American Revolution. This dominance was displaced in the nineteenth and twentieth centuries by the view that freedom indicated a lack of impediments to action, or non-interference (Skinner 2025, especially chapter 9). Although eclipsed in many aspects of public discourse, the independence paradigm persisted within emancipatory groups during the nineteenth century in the United States, notably amongst black writers (Rogers 2023), as well as women's advocates (Coffee 2023) and some labour groups (Gourevitch 2015). Part of the appeal of this model was the revolutionary rhetoric associated with it, expressed powerfully in Patrick Henry's memorable phrase in the build up to America's independence war, 'give me liberty, or give me death!' – a slogan which Jacobs endorses as her own motto (*Incidents*, 86). Although Jacobs repeats these lines in the context of making her own escape, the underlying thought is not simply of personal escape from oppression but of the collective rising up of a victimised people followed by their full inclusion and enfranchisement as equal – and independent – members of a citizen body in whose name the laws of the state would operate. It is towards this rich notion of what it is to be genuinely and fully emancipated, as citizens who play a full part in the life of the community as respected equals that Jacobs strives throughout her book. *Incidents* ends with her coming across an obituary written for her uncle Mark Ramsey, noting that 'they called a colored man a *citizen*! Strange words to be uttered in that region!' (166, Jacobs's emphasis). Though she knows how much remains to be done, that a black person can be a citizen in all the fullness of that word is the ultimate goal of freedom.

2.1 Independence

Independence is the central concept in republican political philosophy. It is both a personal and a collective concept. At the individual level, independent persons are not subject to the controlling power of any other people, but can direct their own affairs. Historically, the state of being independent was often equated with the Latin *sui iuris*, or self-governing, following the use of this term in Roman law (Gaius 1904, 35, Coffee 2025, 65). Independent people, therefore, do not *depend* on the say-so of anyone for how they act. Those who are dependent, by contrast, are under someone else's control, or *alieni iuris* (governed by an external or alien power).

Children are dependent, lacking either the maturity to act responsibly or the resources to maintain themselves. Instead, they depend on their parents or guardians. In the nineteenth century, wives, too, were dependent. Lacking their own legal standing, married women were considered part of a single family unit represented by the husband. This prevented wives from, for example, owning property, controlling their own earnings, entering into contracts in their own name, or bringing legal actions. The paradigm of the independent person was the citizen. In principle, citizens are all equal, with each able to make their own decisions about how to lead their lives subject only to the jurisdiction of the law, which is required to act in their collective interests considering the interests of all the citizens. Citizens are not only governed by the law, but have some sort of representation and input into its provisions.

In its Roman origins, the contrast between independence and dependence was shown most clearly in the distinction between citizens (independent freemen) and slaves. The slaves' condition was said to be essentially one of dependence since they were, by definition, governed by an alien will rather than by their own. The power imbalance between the master and the slave, and the relationship of control, has long served as the principal exemplar of what it meant to be unfree. The master's power is said to be arbitrary, based on the master's own whim and caprice. This contrasts with the non-arbitrary power of the law which is constrained so that it acts only in the collective interests of the citizenry. There is, then, more to being a freeman than simply being able to do whatever one wants (subject to the law). Freemen have a stake in society that slaves lack. Freemen are recognised as members of society, in whose name and interests the nation's laws are framed.

As a status indicating political and social belonging, independence has the further feature of being a resilient ideal. It is not sufficient for freedom as independence that one is not being controlled arbitrarily as a matter of fact. One must be protected against the possibility of such control at any time. Slaves whose masters allow them a great deal of latitude for making their own decisions in daily life, for example, cannot be considered as free in the sense of being independent, since their apparent liberty is enjoyed only contingently – at the discretion of their masters – rather than resiliently by right. As Jacobs knew all too well, slaveholder goodwill can all too readily be revoked. Neither does it matter that a poor freeman may be materially worse off than a pampered houseslave since the freeman retains legal protections against interference. On her trip to England, Jacobs recalled how 'the condition of even the meanest and most ignorant among them was vastly superior to the condition of the most favored slaves in America', adding that 'their homes were very humble; but they were protected by law. No insolent patrols could come, in the dead of night, and flog them at their pleasure. The father, when he closed his cottage door, felt safe with his family around him. No master or overseer could come and take from him his wife, or his daughter' (*Incidents*, 153).

2.2 The Nature of Slavery

The language and imagery of slavery in republican literature gave rise to a distinctive understanding of the nature of slavery. Slaves are not simply people who are forced to work, or who cannot do whatever they wish. Neither is slavery grounded in the fact that people are considered to be property that can be bought and sold. Although both of these are, of course, shocking conditions which slaves deeply resented, they are not what makes a person a slave so much as consequences that follow from being enslaved.

Slavery, then, is equated with being dependent. People can, however, be dependent in a variety of ways, and with a range of severity. Republicans have historically used the word slave to describe many kinds of dependence, even where this stops short of the horrors of chattel slavery. These have included the American revolutionaries, baulking at the idea of being taxed without representation by a monarch who was not constrained to consider their interests. Women campaigning for equal political rights used the same language, as did the impoverished workers who referred to themselves as wage slaves (Coffee forthcoming, Gourevitch 2015). It was not that the revolutionaries, feminists and factory workers considered themselves to be 'treated like slaves' but that in being ruled arbitrarily they were indeed slaves. Equating slavery with dependence in this way, raises a tricky problem for republicans. Dependence comes both in degrees and various kinds. Whether it is right to classify all of these as forms of slavery – bearing in mind the magnitude of what this condition connotes – is an issue that has historically divided republican theorists. Whereas for some, 'true' (i.e. chattel) slavery was merely an extreme form of dependence rather than a distinct kind of condition, others held that the mark of servitude is that one can be bought and sold (Bailyn 1992, 230–319; Skinner 2025, 35–6, 235–6; Coffee 2024).[7]

In one respect, however, the situation of American chattel slaves was qualitatively different from the other kinds of case mentioned earlier. If freemen were recognised as full and legitimate members with a full standing in society, then for the various categories of dependent white people – revolutionary militiamen, women, the working poor – while they may have been hugely exploited in their societies, there was a path by which they could achieve enfranchisement. Ending coverture and granting suffrage may not have fully closed the gender gap, for example, but women are considered full citizens, nonetheless. Black slaves did not have this

---

[7] This is not an issue I can settle in this Element. However, as I make clear in footnote 1, I regard chattel slavery as a distinct form of dependence (or domination). American slavery not only consisted in the making of property out of people, but was also situated in a rigid racial caste system that had no conceptual space for black freedom. This said, I do accept that there can be theoretical merit in applying the term 'slavery' to a range of oppressed conditions – particularly in historic contexts such as Mary Wollstonecraft's language of slavery with respect to women's subjection. Wollstonecraft's use of the term slave is not metaphorical but both literal and philosophical, according to what was then its accepted meaning. Accordingly, the term *slave* cannot be removed from her analysis without altering its message (Coffee 2025). Wollstonecraft was aware of the horrors of West Indian plantation slavery, which she regarded as barbaric, while still drawing parallels with the case of English women. In my view, we can recognise different kinds of subjection as 'domination' and 'slavery' without thereby conflating them. Each kind may require its own analysis and redress.

possibility. Manumission did not bring citizenship but an uncertain status as freedmen who lacked the legal and social standing of free whites. They were not members of an economic or social class like the working poor, but of a fixed racial caste. There was an important sense in which black people could never be free in the United States. Fugitive slaves, for example, were not free simply because they had eluded their masters' clutches. They were, rather, slaves on the run, and fair game to the hunters. As we shall discuss in section 5, black freedmen were often in a situation little better, finding that their legal rights were not respected, well-paying work was virtually impossible to come by, and there was always a risk of violence from a hostile white community. As a former slave, Douglass described this condition as slavery, little different from his old life. Deeply entrenched and vicious social prejudice created 'invisible chains of slavery' that continued to bind black Americans 'long after his iron chains are broken and forever buried out of sight' (Douglass 1976, vol 3, 292). Elaborating more fully, he writes

> The workshop denies him work, and the inn denies him shelter; the ballot-box a fair vote, and the jury-box a fair trial. He has ceased to be the slave of society. He may not now be bought and sold like a beast in the market, but he is the trammeled victim of a prejudice, well calculated to repress his manly ambition, paralyze his energies, and make him a dejected and spiritless man, if not a sullen enemy to society, fit to prey upon life and property and to make trouble generally (Douglass 1976, vol. 4, 344).

In both *Incidents* and her letters, both before and after legal manumission and political emancipation, Jacobs describes the same experience and felt equally crushed (§5.5). To give just one illustration – one Jacobs relates almost in passing, but which had the most upsetting consequences for her as a mother – while on the run in Boston, her son Joseph had found work as an apprentice at which he was faring very well. 'He was', she says, 'liked by the master, and was a favorite with his fellow-apprentices', until that is, they 'accidentally discovered a fact that they had never before suspected – that he was colored!' (*Incidents*, 153). At once, this 'transformed him into a different being'. Although Joseph was very light skinned and had facial features not marked out as African American ('he was so entirely white, that he always passed for a white man', Child reports), to the apprentices, 'it was offensive to their dignity to have a "nigger" among them, after they had been told that he *was* a "nigger"'.[8] This treatment was too

---

[8] *Papers*, 680; *Incidents*, 153, Jacobs's emphasis. Child's remarks come in a letter written to an Anglican minister in Australia, appealing for information about Joseph's whereabouts. After money Jacobs sent for her son's passage home went missing, she feared that 'he has been robbed and murdered'.

much for Joseph's pride. He went off to sea, and later followed his uncle to California and Australia, where Joseph eventually died. Jacobs's dream of one day living with her two children was over.

2.3 The Value of Independence

Historically, freedom as independence has been regarded as having immeasurable value. Freedom was the natural, God-given condition of human beings, and accordingly regarded as an expression of one's humanity, to be guarded as preciously as life itself.

As the denial of freedom, then, slavery served to 'imbrute' a person. Richard Price, whose work influenced the discourse of the American Revolution, for example, speaks of 'that sacred blessing of liberty, without which man is a beast' (1991, 68). Mary Wollstonecraft, uses similar language throughout the *Vindication of the Rights of Woman*, arguing that if women 'are really capable of acting like rational creatures, let them not be treated like slaves; or, like the brutes who are dependent on the reason of man' (1992, 61–2). Abolitionists – and in particular, the slaves themselves – also made much of the dehumanising aspect of slavery, with Douglass insisting emphatically that 'the grand aim of slavery ... always and everywhere, is to reduce man to a level with the brute' (*Bondage*, 32). Jacobs makes the same observation. Speaking specifically of female slaves, she writes that 'women are considered of no value, unless they continually increase their owner's stock. They are put on a par with animals' (*Incidents*, 45). Her brother, John, gives what is perhaps the most damning analysis of the dehumanising logic of slavery:

> Take one who has never felt the sting of slavery, he would naturally suppose that it was to the slaveholder's advantage to treat his slaves with kindness; but the more indulgent the master, the more intelligent the slave; the more intelligent the slave, the nearer he approximates to a man; the nearer he approximates to a man, the more determinate he is to be a free man; and to argue that the slaves are happy, or can be happy while in slavery is to argue that they have been brutalised to that degree that they cannot be considered men (Despots, 31).

Such was the value of freedom that its defence became a rallying call, as we noted earlier with Patrick Henry's slogan, preferring death to the usurping of one's liberty. Jacobs reiterates the point, saying explicitly that she would have chosen her life in the garret over her 'lot as a slave' (*Incidents*, 98). In the appendix to *Incidents*, Post quotes Jacobs's words soon after having had her freedom purchased: 'I thank you for your kind expressions in regard to my freedom; but the freedom I had before the money was paid was dearer to me', adding that

> God gave me *that* freedom; but man put God's image in the scales with the paltry sum of three hundred dollars. I served for my liberty as faithfully as Jacob served for Rachel. At the end, he had large possessions; but I was robbed of my victory; I was obliged to resign my crown, to rid myself of a tyrant (168, her emphasis).[9]

In placing an absolute value on her freedom, Jacobs makes clear that there can be no compromise on that status, even if it were to make little practical difference to how one was treated, or perhaps made life a little easier. We see this in her reaction to the letter she received, ostensibly from her old mistress but actually from Norcom. 'You were never treated as a slave', he wrote, 'you were never put to hard work, nor exposed to field labor. On the contrary, you were taken into the house, and treated as one of us, and almost as free; and we, at least, felt that you were above disgracing yourself by running away' (143). Although she smelt a trap, Jacobs' reaction illustrates that slavery is not a matter of how hard one is worked or how badly treated one has been. She works hard anyway and has endured more than almost anyone can imagine. What is at stake is the recognition of human dignity. One cannot, then, be 'almost as free' as a freeman, since the status of slave is necessarily degraded. Once again, John Jacobs expresses the issue with great clarity. Recalling the comparatively comfortable condition he had as one of Sawyer's trusted hands, he justified his desertion: 'but where a man is denied nothing, and entrusted with everything – denied nothing, did I say? He is denied the only thing that could justify him in betraying such trust, that is his liberty, the fountain of all our joy, without which we are the most miserable of all created beings' (*Despots*, 50).

Even when the stakes are not as high as escaping bondage, Harriet insists that it is always better to remain independent than to fall into the power of another, no matter how apparently benign they might be. It was a great boon to Hannah Pritchard – James Norcom's aunt-in-law, and the woman who manumitted Molly Horniblow – to have her own financial security: 'she had enough to be independent; and that is more than can ever be gained from charity, however lavish it may be' (78).

---

[9] In Genesis 29, Jacob serves Laban for fourteen years in order to win the hand of Rachel in marriage.

2.4 The Resilience of Freedom and Its Benefits

Alongside its intrinsic value, there are practical advantages to being independent. These flow from the fact that independence is said to be a resilient condition in that one's status is enshrined in law. Philip Pettit identifies three specific disadvantages that come from being dependent (or as he calls it, dominated). First, domination creates a high degree of uncertainty in one's life (Pettit 1997, 85–6). Secondly, dominated people need to 'keep a weather eye on the powerful, anticipating what they will expect of you' (86). Finally, dominated people are often compelled to 'bow and scrape', currying favour with those with power over them (87).

Jacobs recognised each of these. From the age of twelve, she was confronted by the bitter truth that no promise made to a slave need ever be kept. Until that point, she had felt 'as free from care as that of any free-born white child' (*Incidents*, 11). Those days were, however, 'too happy to last' and 'there came that blight, which too surely waits on every human being born to be a chattel' – the death of an owner. This is not, of course, out of love, or of loyalty to the slaveholder, but because of the uncertainty of what would happen next. Slave families were often broken up. In Jacobs's case, she believed that a promise had been made to free her and her brother. Instead, Jacobs was bequeathed to her mistress's five-year-old niece, Mary Matilda Norcom. Jacobs would never get over this act of betrayal, although she otherwise had kind words for her mistress, Margaret Horniblow. In reality, Horniblow may possibly have kept her promise – Yellin suggests that James Norcom like intervened in his capacity as executor (2004, 15) – although this would have made no practical difference to Jacobs. Slaves come to realise that such manipulation is all too common, and they are powerless to respond.

Jacobs never recovered from her sense of insecurity and betrayal. Recalling her time in hiding, she wrote that 'always I was in dread that by some accident, or some contrivance, slavery would succeed in snatching my children from me' (*Incidents*, 126). Later, when making her escape to the north by sea, the honest captain remarked that he was sorry that Jacobs had so little confidence in his reliability. 'Ah', she reflected, 'if he had ever been a slave he would have known how difficult it was to trust a white man' (133). Later still, Jacobs felt compelled to decline an offer of help from her kind employer, because 'the old feeling of insecurity, especially with regard to my children, often threw its dark shadow across my sunshine' (141).

This last episode was also an illustration of Jacobs's continual need to 'keep a weather eye open', always conscious of how others might react.

She declined the offer because she feared it might upset Sawyer's cousins ('their knowledge of my precarious situation placed me in their power; and I felt that it was important for me to keep on the right side of them'). John Jacobs describes in some detail how distasteful but necessary the process of continually humouring and placating others is to a slave.

> 'When I met Mr. Sawyer, I saluted him as my master. It came rather hard for me to "master" a man, and act the deceitful part of a slave, to pretend love and friendship where I had none ... I did everything That I could to please my present master, who treated me with as much kindness as I could expect from anyone to whom I was a slave' (Despots, 40).

It is imperative to the slave not only to appease his or her master, as Pettit describes, but also to learn to read and understand them with near certain accuracy. In the same chapter, John describes how carefully he learned to read his master's ways, saying of Sawyer's brother, 'I had made a study of the old doctor's ways so long that I really thought I could sometimes tell what he was thinking about' (*Despots*, 42).

2.5 Virtue and Corruption

Independence is not only about the resilient capacity to act. It is also bound up closely with an ideal of virtue. Liberty, to paraphrase John Milton, is not licence ('None can love freedom heartily but good men; the rest love not freedom but licence', 1991, 3). Although independent people are authorised to act as they see fit within the provisions of the law, they are expected to do so responsibly and with restraint. In particular, freemen are supposed to display the norms of civic virtue – those forms of behaviour which will allow the republic to survive and flourish. These include, placing the common good above their private interests, respecting the law, and taking part in public discourse about political matters. The capacity for virtue was not thought to come easily. Rather, a virtuous character was held to result from suitable education and training. Significantly, true virtue could not be simply taught but had to be practiced in order to develop. The condition of dependence was considered to be incompatible with developing virtue, since dependent people cannot practice making sound judgements, but instead must either follow directions or placate those with power over them.

In republican theory, slaves were considered to lack virtue entirely. This was, in part, a conceptual claim since being under someone else's arbitrary power was held to be incompatible with the requirement that virtuous people should always act on principle (the master's word was the slave's law, not the slave's conscience). It was also an empirical commitment based on the slave's lack of moral training and opportunities to develop a virtuous character. One stereotype, going back to Roman times, was that of the cunning and obsequious slave who could be very dangerous. Another stereotype was of the stupid but loyal slave, indolent and lacking in any initiative. This latter was not only a stereotype held by slaveholders but was sometimes an appearance adopted by slaves themselves as a form of defence (*Bondage*, 202–03, Coffee 2020, 61). Not only did slaves lack any formal education, other than what was necessary to perform their duties – Jacobs, recall, was fortunate in being able to read – but they were indoctrinated with an impoverished religion that emphasised only the virtue of obedience. All this presented a significant obstacle to the public's conception of a black citizenry. Since slaves could not conceivably have developed the necessary virtues, they were held to be unsuited to fulfil the rigorous demands of responsible citizenship.

Against this background, it is noticeable that from the very start of *Incidents*, Jacobs emphasises the independent spirit and moral backbone of her enslaved relatives, drawing attention to their moral fortitude, self-reliance, intelligence, diligence, initiative and hunger to educate themselves, and that she ends with the poignance of Ramsey's being considered a good citizen. In spite of their bondage, these are all admirable people, fully worthy of that exalted condition from which they have been debarred.

A second noticeable emphasis is how slaves wrestle with moral dilemmas that might not trouble us today. Jacobs gives the example of Luke, a sexually abused slave from Edenton whom she later recognised in New York. When his abusive master had died, Luke hid some of his master's money in a pair of old trousers, asking the relatives if he could keep them as a memento. He proudly told Jacobs, 'I didn't *steal* it; dey gub it to me' (*Incidents*, 159–60, original emphasis). She explains, 'this is a fair specimen of how the moral sense is educated by slavery. When a man has his wages stolen from him, year after year, the laws sanction and enforce the theft, how can he be expected to have more regard to honesty than has the man who robs him?', adding that 'I agree with poor, ignorant, much-abused Luke, in thinking he had a *right* to that money, as a portion of his unpaid wages' (160).[10] Slaves, then, should not be judged by the laws or moral standards of the slave system. In a defiant reversal of the Supreme

---

[10] John Jacobs gives a similar analysis of his own internal wrestling with the ethics of rebellion (*Despots*, 40–50, §1.2).

Court's infamous phrase regarding Dred Scott, Jacobs declares that she regards the slavery 'laws as the regulations of robbers, who had no rights that I was bound to respect' (155). Her words applied as much to the ethos and moral hypocrisy of slavery as to the legal framework itself. Far from being incapable of virtue because of their condition, Jacobs shows that through resistance, enslaved people develop, nurture and assert their moral dignity, not just as individuals but as families and friends ('there are no bonds so strong as those which are formed by suffering together', 142).

The republican claim that dependence impairs or corrupts virtue cuts both ways. It is not only the condition of dependence that is corrupting but the relationship of dependence. It follows, therefore, that it is not only the dominated whose virtue is debased, but also their dominators. In everyday language, the thought is that 'power corrupts, and absolute power corrupts absolutely'. Not surprisingly, Jacobs makes a great deal of this aspect of the principle in her analysis. In particular, it is the absolute power of the slaveholder over his slave women ('made to obey his command in *every* thing', 19, also 27, 47) and in their marriages that inevitably corrupts their morals. This last matter concerning the pervasive sexual abuse of slaves by men regarded within the community as morally upstanding is the source of Jacobs's most damning criticism. It is, as we noted earlier, inextricably woven into the power structure of the slave system. The moral implications, according to Jacobs, are far-reaching. 'No pen', she laments, 'can give an adequate description of the all-pervading corruption produced by slavery' (47). While the point is a general one, she makes it in the context of the rampant sexual violation of slaves, including the effect that this has on the slaveholders and their own families. 'Had it not been for slavery', she writes regarding a man who has behaved atrociously – to his wife, his slave, and the slave children he has fathered – but who seems to be nobody unusual in that, 'he would have been a better man, and his wife a happier woman'. We will discuss this in greater detail in section 5.

It is not just individual slaveholders that are corrupted. The moral degradation spreads from the plantation to infect the entire society that makes slavery possible, including in the supposedly free North, where she 'found the same manifestations of that cruel prejudice, which so discourages the feelings, and represses the energies of the colored people' (146). The passing of the Fugitive Slave Law brought this tacit hypocrisy out into plain sight, when black men were 'given up by the bloodhounds of the north to the bloodhounds of the south' (157).

3 Agency, Dignity and Virtue

3.1 Slavery's Great Contradiction

There are likely many contradictions in the institutionalised practice of slavery. The most fundamental, as I see it, is as follows. At the formal level, the relationship between free society and the slave population is one between humans and non-human objects: slaves are treated as if they either lack certain distinctively human capacities – rational agency and meaningful emotions – or, if they do possess them, they are deemed morally irrelevant. At the practical level, however, daily interactions between slaveholders and slaves – who of necessity live and operate in very close proximity – are only possible because they are relations between thinking, feeling persons, or human beings. The institution, therefore, simultaneously denies and presupposes the humanity of slaves, giving rise to a fundamental contradiction.[11] This is a prominent theme running through *Incidents*.

When a group of people is made into the personal property of others, a cleft is opened up in society, creating a theoretically unbreachable divide between two castes.[12] It is impossible for the members of either group to treat those in the other as human beings. Those in the higher caste regard those in the lower as subhuman, since this justifies owning them. On this unequal basis, those in the lower caste cannot act towards the others as humans, since this is not how their interactions will be received. At the same time, the members of both castes must engage with each other on a daily basis, living and working alongside each other, communicating face to face. Human interaction being what it is, most of the time these people do in fact treat each other as human beings, relating in a personable way and forming – to varying degrees – mutual understanding, sympathy and even affection. While this allows day-to-day life to function, it is an illusion and there can be no substance behind these emotions. The structural imbalance that exists between the groups, and the logic of how to survive within the system, mean that anyone who crosses the divide to engage with the other side must, at the appropriate moment, disregard any emotion or personal loyalty and act with calculating and callous self-interest. This

---

[11] This contradiction arises irrespective of whether it involves social belief (where the free population genuinely believes that slaves are subhuman) or whether it serves as a practical solution (where a social myth arises to support the institution).

[12] Though a small number of people do move out of the lower caste, they do not make it into the higher. As I discuss below, they exist in an unstable condition closer to the lower than the higher.

dynamic creates a tremendous psychological dissonance that slaveholders, slaves, and members of the broader community often find both confusing and troubling. And yet survival depends on its being upheld – the survival of the system on the part of the slaveholders, the survival of the nation for all white Americans, and daily physical survival for the slaves and free black Americans.[13]

I have set the contradiction out in abstract, rather than moralised, terms since my purpose is only to lay bare the inherent tension that arises when human beings – whose means of both self-understanding and interpersonal communication are predicated on treating their interlocutors as rational and moral agents – operate within a system which formally denies this basic condition, declaring one group to be the livestock of another. Unquestionably, the moral guilt for devising, implementing, and ruthlessly enforcing the institution rests entirely with the dominant group, which, in this case, is the broader white American society that permits and perpetuates it.

It may sound strange that I've referred to a cleft in 'society' when slaves might seem to be better thought of as having been placed deliberately and squarely outside of society, being without the freedom, rights, opportunity, or status to operate within it. From one perspective, this is clearly correct. On the other hand, Jacobs's story is concerned with the extensive and complex relations that slaves had with white Americans, as their masters and within their communities. Jacobs's father was, for example, a respected local carpenter, trusted to hire out his own time, and her grandmother was popular locally, earning money from the sale of her much sought-after cakes. The dream of Jacobs's life was not to leave or overthrow America, but to live within it: 'to sit with my children in a home of my own' (*Incidents*, 166). That she wanted to live within American society is not to deny the extent to which she worked for it to be radically reformed. She did so, however, from within, as someone who felt herself rightfully to be part of that society.

Jacobs's dream was never realised. The apparent freedom of manumission was a mirage. The legal framework of slavery was not the only element in the cleft referred to above. What justified the enslavement of other human beings was its racial basis. This hybrid legal-racial nature gave slavery a logically unstable character. Since slavery was associated with

---

[13] Although some of Jacobs's analysis of the relationship between slaves and masters may evoke and find an echo in aspects of Hegel's famous dialectic, I do not pursue those here. Since Jacobs's work was developed independently, born of experience and observation rather than theory and speculation, I prefer to treat her ideas on their own terms.

blackness, all free black people – no matter whether free born, manumitted, or emancipated by proclamation – were stained with the stigma of servility that is associated with their race (Coffee 2024, 558). As Jacobs found to her cost, even free African Americans experienced a level of prejudice that undermined whatever legal rights they possessed and so severely hindered their social participation as to negate their nominally free status. Freedmen cannot become white, so even if they pass the legal test for freedom, they cannot breach the social barrier.

This sentiment comes across clearly in Jacobs's narrative and letters. However, unlike Douglass, she does not go on to claim explicitly that all African Americans were inescapably enslaved, whether or not in chains. The black man, he argued, 'was free by law, but denied the chief advantages of freedom; he was indeed but nominally free; he was *not compelled to call any man his master, and no one could call him slave*, but he was *still in fact a slave, a slave to society*, and could only be a hewer of wood and a drawer of water' (1979: vol. 5: 619; emphasis added). We will return to this problem in section 5.

The fundamental tension identified earlier exposes the arbitrary basis of any racial division. The servile caste is reserved exclusively for those of 'African' descent ('they seem to satisfy their consciences with the doctrine that God created the Africans to be slaves', *Incidents*, 41). But, Jacobs asks, 'who *are* Africans? Who can measure the amount of Anglo-Saxon blood coursing in the veins of American slaves?' Jacobs herself certainly had both kinds of blood. While she was sometimes taken as having Mediterranean heritage, her children were able to pass as white. The brute fact was that the races mixed, and children were born. Their status had to be determined. As Jacobs notes, both bitterly and wryly, the legal convention held that children born of slave women were also slaves. The slaveholders, she mocks, 'have been cunning enough to enact that "the child shall follow the condition of the *mother*," not of the *father*, thus taking care that licentiousness shall not interfere with avarice' (69, also 39, 157). While this is an optimal outcome for male slaveholders, everybody else – their wives, female slaves, and their own resulting children – loses. There is certainly a financial motive underpinning this arrangement (slave 'women are considered of no value, unless they continually increase their owner's stock. They are put on a par with animals', 45, also 55). However, while their 'stock' may increase in the short term, as the colour of the children grows paler over the generations – as Jacobs highlights – this comes to undermine the racial basis of slavery itself. Louisa Picquet, for example, was legally black as an 'octaroon' (having only one-eighth African ancestry) but white in appearance.

The slaveholders would not be able to pull this contradiction off without the wider population sharing the prejudice that the slaves were something less than fully human ('it had never occurred to Mrs [Norcom] that slaves could have any feelings', 123). Prejudice and profit operate together to sustain slavery. Jacobs identifies both but does not explicitly bring them together, unlike Douglass, who writes: every white 'man who had a thousand dollars so invested had a thousand reasons for painting the black man as fit only for slavery. Having made him the companion of horses and mules, he naturally sought to justify himself by assuming that the Negro was not much better than a mule' (1976, vol. 3, 348).

Wherever slaves and slaveholders interact, its fundamental contradiction can be seen. Slaves are treated as if they have no agency or virtue, and yet when a slaveholder cannot compel them, they are reasoned with or appealed to morally. In an environment in which Norcom has fathered at least eleven children with his slaves, for example, he tells Jacobs how she has 'lowered' herself by giving herself to Sawyer (*Incidents*, 67). Norcom's letter to Jacobs attempts to persuade her to return home, appealing to friendship, expressing sympathy, recounting sadness at the death of Molly Horniblow, and forgiving Jacobs for her disgrace in running away (§2.3). Although the letter was a transparent ruse, its moral and rational tone betrays their realisation that Jacobs is no chattel but a human moral agent. The way John Jacobs walked away from Sawyer illustrates the point from the converse perspective. John accepts that they had mostly got along well and he liked Sawyer as a man. Such feelings, however, had to be put aside. John was not a man in this relationship, but property. He must not, therefore, treat Sawyer as a man. The slave system left him no choice but to play the game ruthlessly and abscond.

Perhaps the clearest instance of slavery's contradiction comes in the fact and extent of the sexual abuse and exploitation that Jacobs identifies as integral to the system. As property, slaves are there to be used in whatever way the master sees fit ('made for his use, made to obey his command in *every* thing', 19, Jacobs's emphasis). Absolute power and male lust combine to make rape inevitable. Norcom, however, does not and cannot see it as rape, and still less as an act of bestiality with his livestock. Instead, he wants Jacobs to desire him, submitting willingly just as any white woman he might have pursued. In short, Norcom interacts with Jacobs alternately – and often simultaneously – as a human being *and* as a dehumanised piece of property. But he cannot have it both ways.

3.2 Independent Citizens in the Making

> My father was a carpenter, and considered so intelligent and skilful in his trade, that, when buildings out of the common line were to be erected, he was sent for from long distances, to be head workman (Incidents, 9).

This is only the second sentence of Jacobs's narrative. Already, she has established that her father, Elijah Knox, was an intelligent, accomplished and respected member of the local community. She goes on to describe his success in building up his own client base in a successful small business, from which he supports himself and puts aside savings. What Jacobs has portrayed is an independent and virtuous citizen. Except, he is a slave.

Knox pays his mistress $200 a year for the privilege of hiring out his own time. Out of this, he must support himself before saving anything for lean times. His lifelong ambition was to purchase his children. This was no small ambition. The fee exacted by his mistress was steep and his working privileges could have been revoked at any time. A typical annual income for a carpenter at that time ranged from $250 to $500 (U.S. Bureau of Labor Statistics 1934, 164–5). If we assume that Knox was fairly successful, he might still have been paying his mistress 40–50% of his earnings. It was a lucrative arrangement for the mistress. To put the fee in the context of the price of slaves, Jacobs's strong and healthy uncle, Joseph Horniblow, was auctioned for $720 (10). Impressively, however, Jacobs records her father as having made several offers to buy her and her brother, all of which were declined.

Both Jacobs's parents died before she was in her teens and so her grandmother was the most important figure in Jacobs's life, a source of emotional support, practical advice and moral instruction. Molly Horniblow, too, is described as intelligent and resourceful. She was trusted to manage the household and hotel of the owners, and permitted to sell her homebaked cakes as a side-business on the condition that she clothe herself and her children from the proceeds. As with Knox, her goal was to purchase her children. And here again, Jacobs portrays her as an independent and virtuous citizen, someone who would be an asset to society rather than a drain on the state. Horniblow was popular locally, and her cakes sold well. Again, like Knox, her efforts to redeem her children were thwarted. When she had saved $300, her mistress asked to borrow the money, promising to repay the loan soon. She never did. That the loan was not repaid is another instance of the contradiction in the slave relationship: superficially, slave and mistress interact as human beings in a convivial and straightforward manner, making a voluntary moral agreement. In reality, however, there are no moral – and certainly no legal – obligations between them: 'a slave, *being* property, can *hold* no property. When my grandmother lent her hard earnings to her mistress, she trusted solely to her honor. The honor of a slaveholder to a slave!' (10, Jacobs's emphasis).

In the end, Jacobs's grandmother achieved some measure of vindication. Molly Horniblow had been promised her freedom by her mistress, Elizabeth Pritchard Horniblow, when she herself died. Although it seems that she kept her promise (something which all too often did not happen), James Norcom – the executor, once again – demanded that Horniblow be sold to pay the estate's debts. He intended to do this quietly, ostensibly to save her the public humiliation though she realised he was really protecting his own reputation. Horniblow knew the affection in which she was held locally: 'if he was base enough to sell her, when the mistress intended she should be free, she was determined the public should know' (*Incidents* 14). Horniblow insisted on standing on the auction block along with her son, Mark Ramsey. The tactic paid off. 'On the appointed day', Jacobs recounts, 'the customary advertisement was posted up, proclaiming that there would be a "public sale of negroes, horses, &c.". The members of the crowd knew of the promise to free her "and every body who knew her respected her intelligence and good character"'. They began to call out, 'Shame! Shame! Who is going to sell *you*, aunt Marthy? Don't stand there! That is no place for *you*'. In the end, nobody bid for Horniblow until the end when someone offered a mere $50, and promptly freed her.[14]

Just as Jacobs opens *Incidents* by demonstrating the potential that slaves had to become independent and virtuous citizens, so she closes the book by observing that this is just what they had become. As we noted in section 2, on the final page Jacobs describes coming across her uncle Mark's obituary (the only time she ever recalled such a notice for a black man), in which he was described as a 'good man and a useful citizen' (166). Although she describes these as 'strange words' to come out of North Carolina, they represent a vindication of her arguments. Black people, including slaves, have shown themselves worthy of citizenship. Although Jacobs does not deny the need for extensive programmes for education and training – as her work in Washington D.C. and Alexandria shows – she does debunk

---

[14] Yellin gives a fuller picture. Molly Horniblow (Aunt Marthy in the text) had given the money to her mistress's sister, Hannah Pritchard, who was to purchase Horniblow and her son, Mark Ramsey, and then to manumit them both. Horniblow was emancipated, although the law required her to take ownership of Ramsey as collateral. State regulations compelled manumitted slaves to prove that they would not burden the state (2004, 21–2).

two widely held myths: that African Americans were incapable of acting independently; and that slavery inevitably and irrevocably renders a person unfit for civic life.

3.3 Dignity and the Love of Liberty

> 'Northerners know nothing at all about Slavery. They think it is perpetual bondage only. They have no conception of the depth of degradation involved in that word, SLAVERY' (Incidents, 3)

This is the opening quotation, printed on the book's title page, and attributed to 'a woman of North Carolina'. It expresses the point made in §2.2 that slavery is not principally a matter of being forced to work, or of not being allowed to do what you want. What wounds slaves most deeply is the inherent degradation of their condition. We can read the quotation in a specific and a general sense. Specifically, 'degradation' has a particular, and horrific, meaning for women that both Jacobs and Child strongly allude to in the preface and introduction to the book. We discuss this more fully in §4.3. More generally, Jacobs considers slavery to be a morally degrading condition, not solely because of the sordid things that might be done to one, but simply as an affront to human dignity. She takes every opportunity to show how slaves manage to maintain their sense of self-worth (her mother, for example, 'had been a slave merely in name, but in nature was noble and womanly', 11).

The indignity of slavery was found not only in dramatic affronts, but in the minutiae of life. Writing her memoir, Jacobs still had the 'vivid recollection of the linsey-woolsey dress' given to her by Mrs Norcom each winter, interjecting: 'how I hated it! It was one of the badges of slavery' (13–14). There was much to dislike about these linen dresses. They were itchy and unflattering. Every teenage girl would also hate wearing such standard issue garments, which is part of Jacobs's point. A slave girl is simply a girl, someone who feels the same emotions as any of Jacobs's readers. Servitude was not anyone's natural condition but was imposed and maintained through daily reminders, both explicit and tacit. That Jacobs hated the badge of slavery reinforces the point that she did not see herself as a slave. Each time she was reminded of it was painful and humiliating – a humiliation that was part of the very purpose of issuing the dresses.

Jacobs regards the love of liberty to be part of the human condition, given by God. That it should ever have had to have been paid for, was a deep and lasting wrong, even if she does accept the practical realities of her situation and closes her book by thanking her friend who 'bestowed the inestimable boon of freedom on me and my children' (166). Although Jacobs endured an unimaginable seven years in the garret in order to ensure that her children would be free, before making her own final flight, she recognises that the relentless and devious propaganda of the slaveholders can be powerful and will blinker some slaves to the blessings of liberty. Lies are told about the degradation and starvation of black people, particularly runaways, in the 'free' north. These lies could be very specific, referring to real escapees – Jacobs heard of one story about someone in apparently dire conditions who was desperate to return home but lacked the courage, only to stay with that person later in New York in comfortable conditions (40). She regrets that some slaves believe these stories and come to regard their present state as the lesser of two evils. Though she understands why they think this way, she believes that with only a modicum of acquaintance with the truth, 'they would know that liberty is more valuable than life. They would begin to understand their own capabilities, and exert themselves to become men and women'.

3.4 Virtue and Agency

As we noted in §2.5, republican theory holds that slaves are necessarily without virtue. This claim was both a conceptual and an empirical commitment. We also noted that the republican model held that it was not only the virtue of slaves that was impaired but the virtue of everyone in a slaveholding society ('I can testify, from my own experience and observation, that slavery is a curse to the whites as well as to the blacks. It makes white fathers cruel and sensual; the sons violent and licentious; it contaminates the daughters, and makes the wives wretched', 48).

Both Harriet and John Jacobs agree that no one – themselves included – escapes morally unscathed from slavery's 'all-pervading corruption' (47). Within this framework, however, they avoid applying blanket stereotypes. Instead, they bring a recognition of human motivation, agency, and reflection as individuals navigate their circumstances, thereby rebutting the abstract claim that virtue and slavery are incompatible. Slaves are no different from the rest of the population: they love their families, have hopes for the future, want security and a better life, and they have moral consciences. Although slaves often find it necessary to make moral compromises, they tend to fare better than their oppressors in maintaining standards ('I do not say there are no humane slaveholders. Such characters do exist. But they are "like angels' visits – few and far between"', 45).[15]

---

[15] The quotation is from Thomas Campbell's 1799 poem, *The Pleasures of Hope*.

Notwithstanding slavery's systemic reach and impact, Jacobs portrays slaves as moral agents responding to their conditions. 'Slavery has not crushed out the animal spirits of these children', she says of the refugees in Alexandria, highlighting their sense of fun and of justice ('they never allow an older and stronger scholar to impose upon a younger and weaker one; and when they happen to have any little delicacies, they are very ready to share') (*Papers*, 559). She also highlights the intense desire to learn and improve themselves displayed by both adults and pupils alike (see §1.4). It made a strong impression on her that the community members wanted black teachers, demonstrating not only their independent spirit but their ambition to develop and progress. It was a spirit Jacobs recognised in herself, recalling her own first arrival in Philadelphia ('every day, almost every hour, I was adding to my little stock of knowledge', *Incidents*, 136–7).

A standard trope in republican discourse is that of cunning, fawning, obsequious slaves who ingratiate themselves with their masters in order to curry favour to win influence or head off danger.[16] It is a crude stereotype, but not without its basis in either fact or the logic of the slave's predicament. Although Jacobs's defiant resistance to Norcom – when he strikes her for talking back, she replies, 'you have struck me for answering you honestly. How I despise you!' (37) – gives the lie to the cliché of the slave as a spineless panderer, she was not above placating the Norcoms when it suited her interests. In the build up to her escape, for example, Jacobs 'did her work faithfully, though not, of course, with a willing mind' in order not to arouse suspicions about her plan (82). What both Harriet and John do, however, is paint a very human picture of slaves strategically weighing up their options. Amongst their great contribution to the republican literature on slavery is that they give the standard assumptions a nuanced, considered underpinning that reflects slaves' individual agency.

John Jacobs gives an especially clear account of how he had to navigate the path between strategic knuckling under and maintaining his own dignity and agency. Even as a young man, he hated addressing the Norcoms as master, particularly when they were children ('I could not make myself believe that they had any right to demand any such humiliation from me', *Despots*, 15). Harriet illustrates John's struggles in a story that he does not himself tell. When John was about 12, one of the young 'masters' used to make stories up about him, using them as a pretext for him to give John a whipping. John would fight back and come out on top. The same young

---

[16] This image stretches back to Ancient Rome. One might think of the comic *servi callidi* (clever slaves) in a number of Plautus's plays, such as Tranio in *The Ghost* (*Mostellaria*).

boy would also rub copper pennies in quicksilver, ordering John to pass them off as quarters on an elderly fruit seller. John was morally troubled: he wanted to inform the seller, but knew that he would be beaten. It was not the pain that he feared, but the indignity of being whipped (*Incidents*, 20). When Harriet advised him that it was always best to do what was right, John responded with a dilemma faced by every slave: 'I try to be good; but what's the use? They are all the time troubling me'.

When John came to be owned by Sawyer, he resolved to hide his bitterness at being a slave, saluting him as master. 'It came rather hard for me at first to "master" a man', he recalls, 'and act the deceitful part of a slave, to pretend love and friendship where I had none' (*Despots*, 40). He adds that 'as unpleasant as it was thus to act, yet under the circumstances in which I was placed, I feel that I have done no wrong'. John worked hard and acquired an impressive reputation for his diagnoses of the sick plantation slaves he was required to visit. His master, he admits, treated him well, even kindly. But he also recognises the sham nature of the slave relationship. John was held against his will and that was decisive (*Despots* 41–2). Later, on a trip with Sawyer to Canada, John saw an opportunity to escape, but was prevented by the knowledge that Harriet and a friend of his were back in Edenton and needed his help. Stopping in New York on the way home, John consults his friends about his dilemma. He asked his friends what his duty was, regarding his escape plan, 'the answer', he writes, 'was a natural one – "look out for yourself first"' (48). Although individual slaves may behave more or less impressively to our eyes as modern readers, the brutal 'morality' that governs the slave system is just as John's friends said: look out for yourself first.

3.5 Why Does the Slave Ever Love?

Any institutional system in which the imperative is to look out for oneself is profoundly isolating. This is not to say that slaves intend to isolate themselves or act selfishly. That is manifestly false. The social structure in which they live, however, undermines the bases upon which sustained and intimate relationships can be built both directly and indirectly. The Jacobs family had as strong a family ethos as one could ever hope for. They loved each other, relied on each other for emotional support and practical help, and stood by each other. And yet, Harriet's Uncle Joseph ran away never to be heard from again, her brother John spent many years prospecting and at sea, and her son Joseph died in Australia in spite of Jacobs's efforts to track him down. Jacobs was herself on the run when her grandmother died back in Edenton. Molly Horniblow's children were each given as wedding gifts within the slaveholder's family, with only good fortune keeping them all local. The threat of Harriet's children being either sold or physically and mentally broken was what prompted her flight.

Aside from the ever-present risk of being sold, or having loved ones sent away, several other factors combined to inhibit slaves' ability to form close relationships. One was the enforced silence concerning the sexually abusive practices that everybody knew took place. Though abuse was an open secret, to speak of it was 'an offence that never went unpunished' (*Incidents*, 28). When her mistress died, Jacobs was taken into the Norcoms' home to work. At a vulnerable time in life – already an orphan – this was a daunting experience, although her aunt Betty was often around. Added to this was the creepy, seedy atmosphere that she was just beginning to understand. One of Jacobs's first memories after moving in was of a desperate slave woman being sold, almost certainly without her child. Norcom told her, 'you have let your tongue run too far; damn you!' (16). She had, Jacobs explains 'forgotten that it was a crime for a slave to tell who was the father' (16).

In all this, no protection was afforded by the slaveholders' wives. 'The mistress, who ought to protect the helpless victim', Jacobs notes, 'has no other feelings towards her but those of jealousy and rage' (27). A girl, she adds, 'will learn, before she is twelve years old, why it is that her mistress hates such and such a one among the slaves. Perhaps the child's own mother is among those hated ones. She listens to violent outbreaks of jealous passion, and cannot help understanding the cause' (28). That said, Jacobs does not condemn the wives so much as the system that produced them. When Norcom's sexual interest in Jacobs became apparent, his wife approached her, saying, 'sit down, look me directly in the face, and tell me all that has passed between your master and you' (32). Although there had been nothing physical, Mrs Norcom's 'color changed frequently, she wept, and sometimes groaned'. Though Jacobs felt sympathetic towards her mistress – she felt 'as other women would under similar circumstances' – she reminded herself that these were the feelings of wounded pride rather than empathy for the victimised girl: 'her marriage vows were desecrated, her dignity insulted; but she had no compassion for the poor victim of her husband's perfidy. She pitied herself as a martyr; but she was incapable of feeling for the condition of shame and misery in which her unfortunate, helpless slave was placed' (32).

Although some of the women in the house, including Aunt Betty, would try strategically to keep Norcom away from Jacobs, the doctor was not deterred. For a teenage girl, Jacobs found the experience frightening, sickening, confusing and humiliating in equal measure. It is hard enough for any victim to speak about abuse, but for slaves with the threat of reprisals to them and their families, it is all the more isolating.

A second reason why Norcom's pursuit of Jacobs was so isolating was that it was a direct assault on her sense of virtue. At such a young age, when a person's values are still developing, the pressure on a girl to violate the 'religious principles inculcated by some pious mother or grandmother', or to betray to 'a lover whose good opinion and peace of mind are dear to her heart' is unbearable, especially given the code of silence that prevents her from talking about her situation (47). Reminding her audience of their own privileges, Jacobs writes, 'O, ye happy women, whose purity has been sheltered from childhood, who have been free to choose the objects of your affection, whose homes are protected by law, do not judge the poor desolate slave girl too severely!' (49). Though acknowledging that, tragically, some women may have been 'too much brutalized by slavery to feel the humiliation of their position', she reminds us that many 'feel it most acutely, and shrink from the memory of it', adding candidly, 'I cannot tell how much I suffered in the presence of these wrongs, nor how I am still pained by the retrospect' (28).

Another way in which slavery undermines relationships is more direct, and supplies the title of this section. While being pursued by Norcom, Jacobs began a consensual and respectful relationship with a free black man. It was her first love. Although she wanted to marry the man, her heart sank at what this would mean. Since 'the laws gave no sanction to the marriage' of a slave, 'the husband of a slave has no power to protect her' from Norcom's lustful clutches (35). Her suitor wanted to buy Jacobs's freedom, but she knew that Norcom would never consent (seeming to think that 'slaves had no right to any family ties of their own; that they were created merely to wait upon the family of the mistress', 35). Jacobs was right. It was when Norcom learned that she who resisted him was in love, not just with another – he asked her that question directly – but with 'a nigger', that he hit her (36). Broken-hearted, Jacobs advised her lover to move to the Free States, which, reluctantly, he did. 'With me', she remembers, 'the lamp of hope had gone out. The dream of my girlhood was over. I felt lonely and desolate' (39).

Two final incidents further illustrate the impossibility of creating a strong and protective family environment. 'One day, when his father and his mistress both happened to call him at the same time' John Jacobs hesitated, not knowing whom to obey; finally choosing to go to his mistress

(*Incidents*, 12). Knox was furious. 'You are my child', he scolded, 'and when I call you, you should come immediately, if you have to pass through fire and water'. John himself remembers his father's words slightly differently, although the effect is the same: 'whenever I call you again, come to me, I care not who else may call … if she is your mistress, I am your father' (*Despots*, 7). This incident, he recalled, made the deepest impression on his mind of his whole life. While Knox yearned to assert his human significance, the reality for 'every slave throughout the United States' was that 'he owns nothing – he can claim nothing. His wife is not his – his children are not his; they can be taken from him, and sold at any minute', adding that 'to be a man and not to be – a father without authority – a husband and no protector – is far pleasanter to dream of than to experience' (6).

When her father died, Jacobs came to understand the resonance of her brother's words, and just how insignificant their lives were to the slaveholders. 'I thought I should be allowed to go to my father's house the next morning', she recalls,

> but I was ordered to go for flowers, that my mistress's house might be decorated for an evening party. I spent the day gathering flowers and weaving them into festoons, while the dead body of my father was lying within a mile of me. What cared my owners for that? he was merely a piece of property. Moreover, they thought he had spoiled his children, by teaching them to feel that they were human beings. This was blasphemous doctrine for a slave to teach; presumptuous in him, and dangerous to the masters (Incidents, 13).

The contradiction in the slave system is once again apparent. In normal daily life, slave and master interact as human beings leading the slaves to forget themselves, only to be brutally reminded in moments like these. The slaves, nevertheless, exerted what agency they could: 'the next day I followed his remains to a humble grave beside that of my dear mother. There were those who knew my father's worth, and respected his memory'.

3.6 Personal Religion

The official religious instruction given to slaves boiled down to one key text: 'servants, be obedient to them that are your masters according to the flesh, with fear and trembling, in singleness of your heart, as unto Christ' (*Incidents* 61, Ephesians 6: 5).[17] The pious representatives of the faith – the slaveholders

---

[17] Where the King James Version has 'servant' for the Greek δοῦλος, modern translations tend to use 'slave'.

and the servile clergymen they employ – are diabolical hypocrites. Jacobs captures both aspects, observing that

> 'if a man goes to the communion table, and pays money into the treasury of the church, no matter if it be the price of blood, he is called religious. If a pastor has offspring by a woman not his wife, the church dismiss him, if she is a white woman; but if she is colored, it does not hinder his continuing to be their good shepherd (67, original grammar).

Earlier in the same chapter, Jacobs recalls attending a church group meeting at which a slave mother was weeping aloud, crying out to God because her children had been sold, she did not know where. The group leader was red in the face, suppressing his laughter – he was a slave trader who had himself whipped members of his own church at the public whipping post (63). Such experiences had given Jacobs a 'prejudice against the episcopal church', whose services seemed to be 'a mockery and a sham', or as she said elsewhere, 'a garb put on for Sunday, and laid aside till Sunday' (153, 46). Though there were some examples of well-intentioned preachers attempting to impart a more Christlike message, their influence was quickly snuffed out.

Against this background, it is striking just how personal a faith Jacobs exhibits. Once more highlighting an inner life so often denied of or ignored in slaves, Jacobs reacts in moments of anguish or self-doubt in ways that any believer today would recognise. As a girl in the Norcom's house, after a number of upsetting incidents that included being made to walk barefoot through the snow and being wrongly accused of lying, Jacobs asked herself, 'for what wise purpose God was leading me though such thorny paths' (21). That is not the thought of a mere slave whose natural or godly purpose is to serve, but of a confused and unhappy purposeful young woman trying to make sense of her life – just as we all do. Later, when she was recounting the story of her thwarted teenage love affair, she writes that 'when separations come by the hand of death, the pious soul can bow in resignation, and say, "not my will, but thine be done, O Lord!" But when the ruthless hand of man strikes the blow, regardless of the misery he causes, it is hard to be submissive' (35). Here again, Jacobs reacts as anyone – especially a youngster – might do when trying to reconcile her hopes and plans with the injustice of her situation in the light of a faith that sometimes seems to demand too much of us.

Jacobs portrays the slaves' faith as more doctrinally sound, and with greater spiritual integrity, than that of the slaveholders. They possess a purer form of religion; one lived personally by believers, each wrestling from within their faith against adversity. They thank God for small mercies and trust him when facing the unknown ('fervently I prayed that God would not forsake me in this hour of utmost need! I was about to risk every thing on the throw of a die', 83, her spelling). While the outward form of Jacobs's religiosity may not be unusual in nineteenth-century literature, in these circumstances her devotion is especially poignant.

4 Feminist Republicanism

Although I place Jacobs in the republican tradition, I do not do so uncritically. Jacobs did not simply make use of conceptual tools she found around her. In writing from her position as a 'slave girl', she modified and adapted ideas as her thoughts developed. In so doing, I argue, Jacobs offers a foundation for a feminist republicanism. I cannot give a detailed account of the feminist debate about republican politics in a short Element (see Bergès and Coffee forthcoming). Instead, I shall follow Karen Green's advice, where she recommends that we read historical women's writing 'on their own terms' and in the context of their production, rather than attributing to them positions drawn from 'a generalisation based on a reading of male-authored texts' (Green 2019, 372).

Jacobs subverts a common set of assumptions that have been both widespread and highly influential in the republican tradition. These assumptions are not, strictly speaking, part of the internal logic of republicanism (Coffee forthcoming). Rather, they represent cultural norms which were prevalent in the societies in which republican ideals were developed, and which were adopted – often unquestioned – by republican theorists and activists. I shall pick out three ideas in particular. The first is that citizenship is an exalted and demanding social position for which those who aspire to attain it must prove themselves worthy. The second is that there is a sharp division between the wretched, subhuman condition of the slave, and the glorious freedom that is an integral part of human dignity. These two ideals were highly gendered and racialised in the nineteenth century and were combined with a third assumption that the exemplar of the independent agent was an individual male.

In the American context, these three principles were almost universally understood – by both scholars and the broader public – in the light of the Revolutionary War. One particular virtue that was not only prized, but often held to be a prerequisite of being qualified to merit the status of citizen, was the willingness to stand up to oppression and injustice – physically resisting domination and, where necessary, being prepared to lay down one's life (Furstenberg 2003). There is a distinctly masculine edge to this principle. Although women have often displayed immense courage in the face of tyranny, they were not considered generally capable of fighting in defence of the nation's freedom. The principle also had a decidedly racialised connotation. White Americans, it was said, had taken up arms against their British oppressors and, against overwhelming odds, successfully claimed their freedom. If black slaves valued their liberty sufficiently, then let them prove themselves by fighting for it. Only then, it was argued, would we have confidence that they had the grit and character to act as freemen and citizens – conveniently setting aside, of course, the fact that very few white Americans had ever been in a position where they had to test their own mettle. White prejudice ignored two clear facts. First, as we noted in §1.4, many contrabands wanted to fight in the Civil War but were rebuffed. Secondly, slave rebellions occurred frequently in the South. Prejudice and propaganda, however, sustained and disseminated the view that the black population either did not want or did not deserve to be free (Blassingame 1972). We return to prejudice and propaganda in §§5.3–6. The onus, therefore, was on each individual slave to show otherwise.

In its widespread and popular form, freedom as independence was articulated in a masculine and white-centred form. When black writers challenged the underlying racial prejudice, they often did so by emphasising black worthiness within what was still a masculine model. A highly influential instance came in Frederick Douglass's telling of his successful physical showdown with a brutal overseer (*Bondage*, 171–82). Douglass's account does not just occupy a central place in discourses about race and slavery but has emerged as a paradigm illustration of independence itself. Because of this, Douglass's fight serves as an excellent foil to highlight the distinctive alternative that Jacobs offers.[18]

Although Jacobs may seem at times to endorse some of the principles outlined earlier, she does this within an overall narrative context that is highly nuanced. The oppressor she faces is not a man with a whip in his hand, but a man that has groomed her from puberty for a sexual abuse that is the norm in her environment. When she resolves to escape, it is not as a lone individual but as a mother whose primary concern is her children's freedom.

---

[18] In contrasting Jacobs with Douglass, I do not criticise Douglass. Personally, I do not consider his overall republicanism as individualist or masculinist, though this episode has often been coopted within the broader republican literature and used as such.

4.1 Frederick Douglass's Transformation

Douglass (1818–95), like Jacobs, was a spirited teenager with an independent streak. Wary of his temperament, Douglass's master decided that he needed 'to be broken', and sent him to spend a year under the authority of a specialist 'negro breaker', Edward Covey (*Bondage*, 149–50). Covey's task was to break Douglass's will. His chosen tactic was to lie in wait before springing out and administering surprise beatings even when the hapless slave was doing what was asked, leaving him feeling that there could be no escape from the constant threat.

After six months, Douglass was 'broken in body, soul and spirit' (160). 'Behold' he says, 'a man transformed into a brute!' He was completely alone, and fully defeated. Contemplating suicide – though not quite ready to die – Douglass makes a decision that would prove transformational. Although he would continue to carry out his duties, he resolved to defend himself if Covey attempted to beat him. Psychologically, Douglass had crossed a line, since not only was it a capital offence to resist a master, it violated the most sacred principle in 'the slave's religious creed' (*Bondage*, 177). It was not long before Douglass's resolve was tested. Covey attacked and Douglass stood firm. 'Whence came the daring spirit', Douglass later wondered, that enabled him to 'grapple with a man who, eight-and-forty hours before, could, with his slightest word have made me tremble like a leaf in a storm' (177). They fought for over two hours, with Douglass emerging victorious. He was never flogged again, by Covey or anybody else.

Douglass describes himself as becoming a changed being: 'I was nothing before; I WAS A MAN NOW. It recalled to life my crushed self-respect and my self-confidence, and inspired me with a renewed determination to be A FREEMAN' (180, Douglass's emphasis). Though still legally a slave, Douglass recalls in a memorable passage:

> After resisting him, I felt as I never had felt before. It was a resurrection from the dark and pestiferous tomb of slavery, to the heaven of comparative freedom. I was no longer a servile coward, trembling under the frown of a brother worm of the dust, but, my long-cowed spirit was roused to an attitude of manly independence. I had reached the point, at which I was not afraid to die. This spirit made me a freeman in fact, while I remained a slave in form (181).

Douglass specifically attributes his rebirth to the fight. Although there were other moments that he could have picked out – such as when he came to realise that resistance was no longer unthinkable – Douglass explains that one 'can only understand the effect of this combat on my spirit, who has himself incurred something, hazarded something, in repelling the unjust and cruel aggressions of a tyrant. Covey was a tyrant, and a cowardly one, withal', continuing just afterwards, 'when a slave cannot be flogged he is more than half free ... While slaves prefer their lives, with flogging, to instant death, they will always find [those like Covey] to accommodate that preference' (180–1).

This, then, was not just any fight but an existential fight against a supreme injustice. Covey was not just a man who stood in Douglass's way. He was a representative of the system that had taken that which made Douglass human – his liberty. Although Douglass had been at rock bottom before the fight, it was not the extent of his wretchedness that diminished his humanity but the nature of his condition. By physically vanquishing his opponent, he had broken slavery's hold on his spirit and reclaimed his manhood. It is a transformation, to coin a slogan, from *servility* to *virility*.

Douglass's fight with Covey has been much discussed (Kohn 2005, Kirkland 2015, Boxill 2018). My concern here, however, is not with Douglass's overall position (which is integrated into his broader philosophy). Rather, my purpose is only to draw out certain features of the story that resonate with the idea that those who deserve freedom must stand up and fight for it. In this story, Douglass rebuts the misconception of the natural servility and cowardice of African Americans. Like Patrick Henry (whom he later quotes), Douglass prefers liberty to death (*Bondage*, 207). Douglass's account, however, upholds the two other common assumptions outlined at the start. Douglass both resists as an individual and identifies a clear moment in which the cowed slave becomes the self-assured freeman.

As a paradigm of someone worthy of freedom, Douglass's portrayal represents a highly masculine image. The heroic individual, unencumbered by family, defies death in a physical struggle, emerging victorious into a new life. Indeed, it is difficult to render Douglass's own phrase – 'I was a man now' – in non-gendered terms whilst retaining his intended rhetorical force. One might, of course, argue that Douglass is simply following the linguistic conventions of his time, rather than specifically invoking an ideal of maleness. This may be correct. Nevertheless, since disentangling gendered assumptions that have been covertly embedded into supposedly abstract ideals of humanity is a notoriously fraught business, I shall retain Douglass's gendered tone in analysing his argument, and will do the same at similar junctures with Jacobs, although I do so with caution.[19]

---

[19] Not everyone accepts the claim that a gender-neutral word such as 'person' cannot be substituted for 'man' without altering Douglass's rhetorical effect, as Laura Brace emphasised to me.

4.2 Slaves Who Dared to Feel Like Men

Before I set out Jacobs's account of her own emancipation, we should note that she does include two episodes in *Incidents* that resemble Douglass's fight, and which make use of some similar language. In a chapter entitled, 'The Slave Who Dared to Feel Like a Man', her uncle, Joseph Horniblow, also physically fights and overpowers his master. This, too, leads to a new sense that there is no going back to servitude ('he said he was no longer a boy, and every day made his yoke more galling. He had raised his hand against his master, and was to be publicly whipped' adding, 'we are dogs here; foot-balls, cattle, every thing that's mean. No, I will not stay. Let them bring me back. We don't die but once', *Incidents* 21–2). Momentous as this event is in Horniblow's life, Jacobs provides very few details, and it plays little part in her narrative as a whole. There is also a key difference between Horniblow's and Douglass's situation. Horniblow was not browbeaten, and he did not come to an awareness of his latent humanity through the conflict. He was already a proud man, someone who detested the idea of slavery more than its hardships. So, while the punch-up galvanised Horniblow, it was not a transformational moment.

Horniblow's fight with his master is not the first story of resistance in the chapter. It follows the incident discussed in §3.4, in which her brother John scuffles with, and bests, his master's son. Again, John is no cringing wretch, but a proud adolescent bristling against a growing awareness of the injustice of his lowly condition. Neither is his fight transformational, but rather the outcome of his growing sense of both self-assertion and frustration. The fight is not a catalyst for his 'becoming a man', but a consequence of it, as he struggles to come to terms with the limitations on his ambitions that every slave must face.

This chapter on 'daring to be a man' is carefully positioned in the narrative, and subtly structured. It follows two introductory chapters that tell of how Jacobs came to be owned by Norcom, and a third chapter that sets the scene for the brutal and arbitrary treatment of slaves on plantations, including the breaking up of families. The chapter also directly precedes the chapter on 'The Trials of Girlhood' which marks the start of Jacobs's own story of abuse, resistance, flight and ultimate victory that occupies the rest of the book. The chapter opens with a contrast between her faithful grandmother's quiet forbearance and strength in accepting God's will in placing them where they were, and the rebellious sense of the injustice of their condition that Jacobs shared with her brother. Jacobs then turns to her own developing troubles with Norcom ('whose restless, craving, vicious nature roved about day and night, seeking whom to devour', 19). Certainly, she feels much of the burning rage and desire to stand strong against such a moral wrong, one that insults her dignity, that her brother and uncle experienced. In reaction to Norcom's 'stinging, scorching words' that scathed her 'ear and brain like fire', she tells us, 'never before had my puny arm felt half so strong' (19). In her retelling, Jacobs here uses a word that she will use twice more to Norcom's face in dramatic fashion, in the coming chapters, 'O, how I despised him!'

Jacobs's own resistance to her enslaved condition is building alongside those of her male relatives. The two male fights – more traditionally recognisable acts of slave rebellion and triumph – provide a backdrop in which she crafts her own specifically female path of defiant overcoming.

The chapter's title is significant. Setting aside its gendered connotations for a moment, the word 'man' may contrast with a number of things, including 'boy' and 'brute'. Douglass, for example, felt himself transformed from a brute to a man. Horniblow, however, already had this status. When he told Jacobs that he was 'no longer a boy', the sense was that he had simply come of age rather than had any particular transformative experience. He had been grounded with a sense of human dignity by his family, as were Harriet and John. This gave them the inner sense of (human) self-worth that Douglass (who felt imbruted) had lacked.

Later, however, while making his escape, Harriet describes how Horniblow's white complexion allowed him to slip away without arousing suspicion. To the white passers-by, Horniblow was a man (a freeman and a citizen) because he was presumed to be white. Had they detected his race, however, Horniblow would have simply been, 'the *thing* rendered back to slavery' (25, Jacobs's emphasis). This, then, introduces another contrast for the term man, that between a freeman (an independent and intentional agent) and a slave (a thing). My claim is not simply that white people treated slaves as if they were things, but that in being denied the use of the essential, God-given quality of independent agency, a thing is what the slave has become, both in their own eyes and the eyes of the white population. Where man refers to 'intentional agent', we can break this down into an internal quality (recognising yourself to be an essentially free, self-asserting being) and an external quality (being recognised as a free agent by others). These two aspects can come apart, so that slaves such as Jacobs and her relatives possessed the first without the second, giving rise to a tragic and destructive tension in one's spirit, one which Douglass referred to as being a freeman in fact but a slave in form.

In daring to feel like a man, then, Horniblow transgressed a rigidly enforced line, one that slaveholders took care to ingrain in slaves' consciousnesses from childhood. Recall how Jacobs was not allowed to attend her father's burial (§3.5). This was not just an act of thoughtlessness or cruelty (though it likely was both). It was imperative that the slaveholders demonstrate that Knox was 'merely a piece of property', as were his children (13). 'By teaching them to feel that they were human beings', they believed, he had spoiled the young Jacobs, since this 'was a blasphemous doctrine for a slave to teach; presumptuous in him, and dangerous to the masters'.

In this context, Jacobs contrasts the non-human condition of servitude with the true humanity that comes from knowing oneself to be worthy of freedom (the inner sense) and thereby acting towards attaining the public standing that this warrants (the outer sense). Discussing the difficulties she had in rousing the spirits of some slaves, so accustomed to the lies and distortions they have received, Jacobs argues ruefully,

> It is difficult to persuade such that freedom could make them useful men, and enable them to protect their wives and children. If those heathen in our Christian land had as much teaching as some Hindoos, they would think otherwise. They would know that liberty is more valuable than life. They would begin to understand their own capabilities, and exert themselves to become men and women (40).[20]

The internal knowledge of their capabilities would spur them on to claim that external recognition of their freedom by others.

By the end of the chapter, the family reflect on the results of their hard efforts. Joseph has arrived safely in New York, Molly Horniblow has been manumitted, with her son Mark all but legally free. They were justifiably proud, telling each other that, 'they would prove to the world that they could take care of themselves, as they had long taken care of others' (27). Their words work both on an individual level – showing that the family had the resourcefulness to prevail as freemen – and on a collective, racial level – the black slaves that waited on others would demonstrate their independence. They concluded by agreeing that 'he that is *willing* to be a slave, let him be a slave'. This is a powerful and provocative slogan, though it is, in my view, best taken as a statement of their defiance and jubilation at a significant moment rather than as a prescription and judgement on those who cannot or do not rebel.

---

[20] When a rare, sincere clergyman was appointed, black people unaccustomed to church began to come, as 'it was the first time they had ever been addressed as human beings' (*Incidents*, 65).

4.3 A Slave Girl's Perspective

Like Douglass, Jacobs will not submit to a moral wrong from her master, she does not fear punishment or even death, and like him, she emerges victorious. Unlike Douglass, however, Jacobs cannot distil the key elements of her experience into a single dramatic episode that marks her transition from slave to freeman, or thing to human. Although it is true that she faced Norcom alone, once she had children she no longer acted for herself. Jacobs's resistance was focussed on the overriding objective of seeing them free before attending to her own needs. And, while she often kept her plans and intentions to herself for practical reasons, the entire manner of her escape was orchestrated and enabled by others. Jacobs's heroic bravery and self-sacrifice were supported by the actions and planning of several other people who were willing to take substantial personal risks.

In framing her story of resistance in the context of sexual abuse, care for family, and reliance on support networks, Jacobs offers political philosophers in the republican tradition an alternative to the individualistic model of civic virtue that is often masculine in form. In §§4.3.1–4.3.3, I focus on her discussion of sexual abuse, before turning to relationships in §4.3.4.

4.3.1 Far More Terrible for Women

> When they told me my new-born babe was a girl, my heart was heavier than it had ever been before. Slavery is terrible for men; but it is far more terrible for women. Superadded to the burden common to all, they have wrongs, and sufferings, and mortifications peculiarly their own (Incidents, 68).

It is hard to comprehend the pervasive, systematic and routine nature of the sexual abuse of female slaves. 'No pen', Jacobs wrote, could give an adequate account of the moral destruction that this wrought (47). If anyone's pen was up to the job, however, it was surely hers. She 'was twenty-one years in that cage of obscene birds', and testifies from her 'own experience and observation' (48). Her insights are so moving and perceptive that this is one section of the Element that is far more powerfully delivered through Jacobs's own words than through any I can add.

One of the most devastating effects of slavery as an institution is that no one who lives within its orbit emerges without being corrupted. 'It makes', Jacobs explains, 'white fathers cruel and sensual; the sons violent and licentious; it contaminates the daughters, and makes the wives wretched. And as for the colored race, it needs an abler pen than mine to describe the extremity of their sufferings, the depth of their degradation' (48). To illustrate:

> The white daughters early hear their parents quarrelling about some female slave. Their curiosity is excited, and they soon learn the cause. They are attended by the young slave girls whom their father has corrupted; and they hear such talk as should never meet youthful ears, or any other ears. They know that the woman slaves are subject to their father's authority in all things; and in some cases they exercise the same authority over the men slaves (47).

Jacobs continues by relating how one slaveholder was humiliated in his neighbourhood because his daughter had deliberately and publicly conceived his first grandchild with 'one of the meanest slaves on his plantation', presumably as an act of rebellion. Though the father was enraged, the daughter emancipated the slave and sent him out of the state.

It was a comfort to Jacobs that her own mother had been spared the violation of her marriage, though she emphasises that while slave vows may be personally significant, they carry no legal force ('she was never in the power of any master; and thus she escaped one class of the evils that generally fall upon slaves', 70). Fortunate as her mother had been in this respect, there was no safe place as a slave. During the reprisals that followed Nat Turner's famous rebellion in 1831, ruthless and brutal searches were made of every slave's home by the local white militias. This was, according to Jacobs, 'a grand opportunity for the low whites, who had no negroes of their own to scourge ... to exercise a little brief authority' (57). They matched the slaveholders for depravity: 'many women hid themselves in woods and swamps, to keep out of their way. If any of the husbands or fathers told of these outrages, they were tied up to the public whipping post, and cruelly scourged' (58).

Jacobs describes what it was like for girls to grow up in this environment. Starting with the general picture, she says:

> The slave girl is reared in an atmosphere of licentiousness and fear. The lash and the foul talk of her master and his sons are her teachers. When she is fourteen or fifteen, her owner, or his sons, or the overseer, or perhaps all of them, begin to bribe her with presents. If these fail to accomplish their purpose, she is whipped or starved into submission to their will. She may have had religious principles inculcated by some pious mother or grandmother, or some good mistress; she may have a lover, whose good opinion and peace of mind are dear to her heart; or the profligate men who have power over her may be exceedingly odious to her. But resistance is hopeless (47).

Although Jacobs herself was not whipped into submission or raped, she speaks from personal experience about the sexual dynamics of asymmetrical power. When she writes about her own situation, she gives us an insight into the process of grooming that began in her early teens, and the psychological methods that Norcom would use to alternately woo her and break her. His jealousy of her romantic attachments is clear – he twice asked her if she loved the man in question (54, 63) – as is his need both for her to respect his complete authority over her and for her simultaneously to desire him as a lover rather than as a master.

4.3.2 Made for His Use

The age of fifteen was, Jacobs tells us, 'a sad epoch in the life of a slave girl' (27).[21] This was when Norcom began to 'whisper foul words' in her ear, telling her that she was 'made for his use, made to obey his command in *every* thing', and emphasising the fact that she 'was nothing but a slave, whose will must and should surrender to his' (28, 19; Jacobs's italics). As 'his property', he added, she 'must be subject to his will in all things' (27). The phrase 'made for his use' was widely understood in this context. It is both euphemistic and understated, while being clear – and sinister – in its meaning.

Norcom spoke in a lewd, suggestive manner to Jacobs – peopling her 'young mind with unclean images, such as only a vile monster could think of' (27). She was all too aware of the age gap and felt trapped ('I was compelled to live under the same roof with him – where I saw a man forty years my senior daily violating the most sacred commandments of nature', 27). She had, however, nowhere to turn. As we discussed in section 3, though Norcom's behaviour towards her was common knowledge, she could never speak about it, in part because of the unbreakable code of silence, but just as much because of the deep shame and disgust that Jacobs felt. Norcom's manner was designed to keep her unsettled, seemingly employing the time-worn abusers' tactic of switching between 'stormy, terrific ways, that made his victims tremble' and 'a gentleness that he thought must surely subdue' (27). Of the two, Jacobs preferred the former, terrifying though it was.

Although Jacobs was valiant in her resistance, she knows that was also lucky. Even if she escaped physical molestation, however, the phrase she

---

[21] Whether it is significant or not, I cannot say, though it is worth noting that Norcom married his second wife, Mary Matilda when she was 15, the same age as Jacobs would be when he started grooming her.

used above that 'resistance is hopeless' was still accurate. Jacobs could not help but be affected by the moral norms around her. Jacobs was a teenager and wanted to do what teenagers do. And so, when another slaveholder, Sawyer, took an interest in her, her head was turned. 'So much attention from a superior person was, of course, flattering; for human nature is the same in all' (48). In the end, and against her better judgement and the ideal of moral virtue that she held dear, Jacobs began a sexual relationship with Sawyer. She understood the nature of their liaison – 'the impassable gulf between them' – but rationalised it to herself:

> to be an object of interest to a man who is not married, and who is not her master, is agreeable to the pride and feelings of a slave, if her miserable situation has left her any pride or sentiment. It seems less degrading to give one's self, than to submit to compulsion. There is something akin to freedom in having a lover who has no control over you, except that which he gains by kindness and attachment. A master may treat you as rudely as he pleases, and you dare not speak; moreover, the wrong does not seem so great with an unmarried man, as with one who has a wife to be made unhappy (48).

Jacobs accepts that 'there may be sophistry in all this', though she reminds us that 'the condition of a slave confuses all principles of morality, and, in fact, renders the practice of them impossible'. As we have noted, Jacobs's two children were fathered by Sawyer.

4.3.3 How I Despise You!

> 'You have struck me for answering you honestly. How I despise you!' ...
> 'Do you know that I have a right to do as I like with you,—that I can kill you, if I please?'
> 'You have tried to kill me, and I wish you had; but you have no right to do as you like with me' (Incidents, 37)

Institutionalised and normalised rape and abuse are not like the beatings to which Douglass stood up. There was no escape for Jacobs. If she resisted one day, Norcom would be back the next. While Covey was humiliated by his defeat, leaving Douglass alone with his reputation in tatters, there was no such release from a seasoned groomer (*Bondage*, 181). Though Jacobs stood up to Norcom, condemning him for striking her and expressing her contempt for him, this did not bring victory. Her position was weakened by her entanglement with Sawyer. Although few readers today are likely to judge Jacobs harshly, in her own eyes she had betrayed herself and let her family down. 'I did not feel as proud as I had done', she recalls, 'My strongest weapon with him was gone. I was lowered in my own estimation' (53). Even then, she manages to reply to the offended Norcom, 'I have sinned against God and myself ... but not against you'.

No show of strength by Jacobs can alter the unequal balance of power with Norcom. And if it were not Norcom who abused her, it would likely have been his son or another rogue. Jacobs's sex marks her out from girlhood as someone who will attract the attention of someone powerful, relentless and likely unstoppable. And though all this is common knowledge, she cannot speak about it. The situation confronting female slaves, then, is qualitatively different from that facing males. The nature of her situation dawned slowly on Jacobs, as she pieced together the clues herself. At an inexperienced age, she realised what Norcom's intentions were, and an uneasy wariness that she developed remained with her as a constant presence. Her fate as a slave girl was one that not even marriage could protect her from, since slave marriages were neither legally recognised nor respected by slaveholders.

Here, Jacobs offers republican theorists a feminist insight. The violent showdown model of resistance is not built into the internal structure of republican thinking. It is an imported, masculine, assumption that Jacobs challenges us to rethink. Though the female slave's situation is more extreme than many women would recognise today – which is not to diminish the abuse that still routinely takes place – the basic sense of the ubiquity and normalisation of being sexualised, the ever-present threat of violation and the horror of what that entails, as well as the supreme priority of maintaining bodily integrity are themes that resonate today. Jacobs shows that republicans can make this perspective foundational, rather than the model of one-off conflict. And, returning to the language of 'becoming a man' from §4.1, it would make no sense for Jacobs to say that she 'became a woman' upon besting, or simply eluding Norcom. She had never been able to forget that she was a woman.

Finally, although our topic has been female sexual abuse, Jacobs is aware that men are also victimised. In a quotation in §4.3.1, speaking of abusive slaveholders, Jacobs records that 'in some cases they exercise the same authority over the men slaves' as they do over the women. Later, she relates the distressing story of Luke, about whom we heard in §2.5. Luke had been made for many years to wait on his bedridden master naked from the waist down, to make it easier for him to be beaten on his buttocks, and to be subject to 'freaks ... of a nature too filthy to be repeated' (156–7). While it is important to acknowledge this reality, it does not change the broader analysis of the inescapability and normalisation of female sexualisation and abuse.

4.3.4 Family, Children and Allies

> I could have made my escape alone; but it was more for my helpless children than for myself that I longed for freedom. Though the boon would have been precious to me, above all price, I would not have taken it at the expense of leaving them in slavery. Every trial I endured, every sacrifice I made for their sakes, drew them closer to my heart, and gave me fresh courage to beat back the dark waves that rolled and rolled over me in a seemingly endless night of storms (Incidents, 78).

In the fight with Covey, the emphasis is squarely on Douglass as an individual. It should be acknowledged, of course, that he does not say that he fought that battle entirely unaided. There were, for example, other slaves watching who were ordered by Covey to assist him, but who refused at great risk to themselves. But the narrative focusses on Douglass's mental state, the actions that he took, and the transformative effect that this had. This contrasts with Jacobs's framing of her narrative, in which concerns for, and assistance from, other people are always in the foreground.

As Jacobs tells Joseph Horniblow's story, it is closer to Douglass's than to her own. Horniblow's final words to his brother were, 'I part with all my kindred', to which Jacobs adds, 'and so it proved. We never heard from him again' (25). Horniblow was not, however, indifferent to his family. When, for example, he was first re-captured, he managed to break away, thinking of drowning himself. Remembering his mother, he stopped himself (23). This said, Horniblow is presented as having an unquenchable yearning to be free, or to die. Jacobs realises this as soon as she has rashly condemned him for abandoning them. 'Go', she blurted out, 'and break your mother's heart', immediately regretting what she had said (22). Horniblow was wounded by his niece's words, but his hatred of slavery and craving for freedom were such that he was compelled to strike out alone.

Though Jacobs's feelings about slavery and freedom were no less strong, her goals are always framed from within her relationships. Her early plans for escape were made with her brother, John ('nothing seemed more dreadful than my present life. I said to myself, "William *must* be free. He shall go to the north, and I will follow him." Many a slave sister has formed the same plans', 40). Once her children were born, Jacobs's thoughts about freedom are entirely focussed on their well-being ('hitherto, I had suffered alone; now, my little one was to be treated as a slave' (75); 'earnestly I prayed that she might never feel the weight of slavery's chain, whose iron entereth into the soul!', 69). Escape without her children is unthinkable. Freedom, then, is not something that Jacobs seeks for herself. It is a shared good that she can only partake of in conjunction with those close to her.

I am not claiming that Jacobs is more concerned with family and children because of her sex. Her uncle Mark was no less tireless and devoted. Although he was effectively free – being formally owned by his own mother – and could have left Edenton at any time, he chose to remain with his mother (Jacobs's grandmother) and was instrumental in helping his niece and her children escape (§3.2). Our concern in this Element is with philosophy rather than biography, and to that end, Jacobs does give us an account that places the individual within a network of relationships. This, I suggest, provides a more effective foundation for a feminist republicanism.

This said, Douglass highlights a significant feature of the slave system, namely that it 'does away with fathers, as it does away with families' (*Bondage*, 41). One reason was that slave children were more likely to be kept with their mothers (though, as we have discussed, this was not always the case). A second reason that Jacobs emphasises repeatedly, is that it was also very common for slaveholders themselves to father slave children that they then disowned. Douglass was one such child. Jacobs's own children were a variant of this theme.

Whatever the specific causes were, the fact was that at similar ages, Douglass was without children, while Jacobs had two. Jacobs also had a supportive network of close family around her that Douglass did not. To the extent that their respective philosophy is tied in with their autobiography – which is the source we are analysing – then it is from this very different starting point that Jacobs develops a more relationally nuanced account of her transition from slavery to freedom.

A second notable aspect of Jacobs's story is the emphasis she gives to the help she receives from others. She is no Lone Ranger fighting her own battles. Of course, she had to stand up against Norcom, and rightly she is celebrated for her feat of endurance, living in a space in which she could barely move, surviving the elements, the tedium, the emotional weight of seven lost years. She showed great personal courage, determination, ingenuity and intelligence throughout. At the same time, it is clear that she could have done none of this on her own. When she first fled from Norcom, she had no plan except that of a friend to conceal her for the time being. Her thought was not to involve anyone else ('I want no one brought into trouble on my account', 84). This strategy did not last long, however. After a week, sensing her pursuers nearby, she hid in some bushes where she was bitten by a snake – likely a copperhead – which required swift attention. She then reaches out to her family, cautiously until as she put it, 'God in his mercy raised up a "friend in need"' (86), in the form of Martha

Hoskins Rombough Blount, the wife of a local slaveholder who herself held slaves in her own name. Blount was a friend of Molly Horniblow, and disapproved of Norcom's antics. Plans were made without involving Jacobs, who was blindfolded and transported to Blount's house where she was secreted for several weeks until it became too dangerous to continue. Jacobs's children and brother were thrust into the local jail – a grim, dank, dingy building which still stands in Edenton, only ceasing to be operational in 1975 – as a reprisal. In the meantime, Ramsey had been preparing the garret space for Jacobs when she was eventually moved from Blount's property.

In laying bare her need for others, Jacobs highlights the relational side of republicanism that is often overlooked where the focus is on personal independence. Jacobs's strong independent spirit is firmly embedded in her reliance on the relationships that were dear to her.

5 Structural Domination

One might imagine that when Jacobs landed in Philadelphia, having finally left her garret, that she was free. That had been Jacobs's expectation, too. She called her companion on the sea voyage North, 'to see the sun rise, for the first time in our lives, on free soil' (133). She immediately qualifies this, however, adding, 'for such I *then* believed it to be' (her emphasis). For one thing, she was still legally a slave and being relentlessly hunted by Norcom. Even that was a comparatively contained problem compared with the extent and virulence of the racial prejudice that she would experience in the North. Significantly, it was not until she visited England – still formally enslaved – that she lay her head on her pillow, 'for the first time, with the delightful consciousness of pure, unadulterated freedom' (151). The reason she gave was that 'for the first time in my life I was in a place where I was treated according to my deportment, without reference to my complexion. I felt as if a great millstone had been lifted from my breast'.

Part of what is required for genuine freedom for Jacobs is to be recognised and treated as a moral, social and political equal. One should, for example, be subject to the same laws, which themselves must treat one equally, and one must have the same opportunities, including access to education, employment and housing. None of these conditions obtained in the North. Although she does not use the same language, her conclusions are similar to Douglass's, who maintained throughout the Reconstruction era that the supposedly freed black population in fact remained enslaved, having merely exchanged 'the relation of slavery to individuals, only to become the slaves of the community at large' (Douglass 1976, 3:292; Coffee 2023). In other words, the social, legal, economic and political reality of life after emancipation combined to keep black Americans in a dependent and oppressed state that was slavery in all but name.

In writing *Incidents*, Jacobs's aim was to 'arouse the women of the North' into both an awareness of the condition of the two million other women like her who still suffered in the South, and to stimulate them into action in bringing an end to slavery (*Incidents*, 5). In order to do that, she would first have to be believed. This was no small task. We have already noted in the introduction how important it was for her book to be endorsed by someone prominent before it could be published. This meant that she would have to convince a famous white person of her credentials. Even after publication, we see Child and Post repeatedly testifying to Jacobs's reliability to potential backers, often by hinting at how nearly white she is. In a letter to Whittier (§1.3), for example, Child describes Jacobs as 'a quick-witted, intelligent woman, with great refinement and propriety of manners', adding that her daughter was stylish and attractive, as white as an Italian (*Papers*, 342–3).

In the next section, we will examine one aspect of the epistemic injustice confronting Jacobs. After that, we will look at the effects of Southern propaganda, both in deceiving and placating the slaves and in sustaining a positive image in the North (§§5.2–5.3), and the structural nature of racism that has proven so resilient not only in Jacobs's own time but even up to our own (§§5.4–5.6).

5.1 Testimonial Injustice: Norcom and the Defence of Hierarchy

Had Jacobs not written her memoir, Norcom might have been remembered for his successful medical practice and charitable work. He studied under Benjamin Rush, one of the signatories of the Declaration of Independence and a leading doctor and psychiatrist whose work was said to 'set the standard of medicine during his day' (Long 1917, 10). While he was by no means a widely known figure, Norcom has retained a degree of prominence in North Carolina's local history. His page in the *NCPedia* – North Carolina's state-run cultural website – is written in glowing terms with only a short reference to his 'licentious' behaviour at the end, with an extract from, along with a link to, Harriet Jacobs's entry (which is, incidentally, two thirds the length of Norcom's bio) (Gass 2022). In 1989, shortly after Yellin's new edition of *Incidents* in which the names of the original protagonists were revealed, the established North Carolina historian, Thomas Parramore, presented a defence of Norcom's character at the joint annual meeting of the North Carolina Literary and Historical Association and the Federation of North Carolina Historical Societies against what he described as Jacobs's 'overwrought and libelous portrait of her former master', published the following year (Parramore 1990, 85). It is worth pausing to examine Parramore's comments, since his view of Norcom's character and of Jacobs's reported remarks – even as recently as the 1990s – shows something of the overwhelming odds against which she struggled to make herself heard and believed.

Parramore starts by praising Norcom's character and achievements, describing him as 'a gifted and tireless medical scientist, perhaps the foremost one in North Carolina during his lifetime', paying tribute to 'his energetic and unremitting concern for his patients' while also remarking that 'in stolen moments amid his demanding schedule, he indulged his love of literature and ancient languages' (82–3). These, Parramore considered to be deductions warranted by the fragmentary but sufficiently clear public record, concluding that Norcom, 'driven by the twin demons of personal ambition and civic obligation ... gave himself unreservedly to the betterment of his community, his state, and his nation' (83). Moving on to Norcom's private life, he finds him to be 'a man of almost fanatically high principles', frequently giving stern but wholesome and uplifting advice to his six children (83). In writing to his future wife, Maria Matilda's mother, Parramore notes – not with any irony – how Norcom exhorts her never to 'suffer yourself to be troubled & tossed about by those giddy & impertinent coxcombs who make it a practice of trifling with little girls' (84). Parramore goes on to discuss how 'the nurturing of such severe standards of conduct for himself and others around him perhaps inevitably filled much of James Norcom's personal life with disappointment and a sense of almost constant betrayal', referring to the nightmare of his marriage to his first wife whose 'addiction to drugs, slatternly and spendthrift comportment, and adultery' drove Norcom, 'to the verge of self-destruction' (84). Parramore also outlines several other conflicts in Norcom's life, including his narrow loss in an election for Edenton's House of Commons which he believed to have been fraudulent, an acrimonious split with his medical business partner, and a contentious resignation from the freemasons. As his standing in the community fell, Norcom believed it was because of his lack of personal wealth. In a letter written shortly before his death, he wrote that 'my life has been a long & painful struggle ... I often wish, that I may someday wake up from my afflicting slumbers & find all which I have experienced, suffered and undergone is a delusion — But no: it is not to be so' (84).

Having noted all this, Parramore turns to Jacobs's allegations. Although Parramore had earlier referenced Norcom's six children, he now notes that Jacobs accused him of having fathered eleven slave children, threatening anyone who might expose him. Parramore also acknowledges that Norcom stands accused of having physically struck Jacobs and inflicting extreme punishments on other slaves – suspending them in mid-air or whipping them over a hundred times – for minor infractions. Parramore does not consider what Jacobs says in any more detail than just to note these points. Instead, he concludes: 'shall we accept the proposition, then, that James Norcom could harbor within his complex personality at once the characteristics of an honorable and dutiful father and those of a perverted tyrant? Of course not, and Harriet Jacobs must stand condemned' for what she has wrongfully said (85). I should reiterate, at this point, that Jacobs has not in fact accused her former master of anything since her publication used pseudonyms throughout. Nevertheless, Parramore considers what he regards as 'the independent evidence' to be 'persuasively, overwhelmingly against her', referring not to any specific exonerating factual evidence but instead to the weight of probability based on his assessment of Norcom's public character and the prevailing norms of Southern slaveholding life.

Parramore does not believe that Jacobs has deliberately perpetrated a hoax. He acknowledges that Norcom might perhaps have been occasionally lewd or suggestive towards an attractive slave girl and so suggests that this may have understandably caused Jacobs to 'suspect and loathe' him, even if it is 'unwarrantable to suppose that there was much more than this strand of truth in the web of alleged deceits and cruelties she spun about him' (86). Based on these conjectures, Parramore suggests that 'Dr. Norcom's moral imperatives may have come into unhappy collision with one another. One of these was that the virtue of women must be respected – no doubt that of a slave woman as much as any other. But another was the obedience owed by the lesser to the greater in a relationship' (86). It is this latter principle that Parramore places most weight upon in his assessment of Norcom. Society 'in the slave South', he notes, 'was rigidly hierarchical; it required the strenuous efforts of Dr. Norcom and his kind to keep it so', adding that 'for slavery, for virtue itself to abide, the social system must remain' (86). Jacobs was Norcom's slave. She was also young, and female. Finally, Norcom saw Jacobs as someone on whom he had generously bestowed privileges, for which she should be grateful. 'That she should spurn his advances', Parramore concludes, 'was not in accordance with the hallowed obligations of the God-appointed Great Chain of Being', so that 'to Dr. Norcom's controllable sensuality were added the virtually irresistible dictates of venerable and sacred hierarchy' (87).

On Parramore's account, Norcom's professional standing and achievements, and his commitment to Southern ideals of hierarchy – social, racial and gendered – give him a high degree of reputational protection. His career and ambition are seen as serving the public, and his external espousal of the accepted principles of religion and discipline, as well as the vigorous insistence on the obedience to rank by subordinates and inferiors, are taken as strong evidence of a virtuous character. For a man at the top of the hierarchy to be accused of such base acts by someone at the very bottom – young, black, female, and a slave – is simply not credible. If she is not malicious, then she is imaginative and deluded.

The epistemic scales, then, have been tipped against Jacobs in two ways as she tries to tell her story. She is not believed because of who she is (just a slave girl) and she is not believed because of what she says (eminent public servants do not behave in this way). In Karen Jones's phrase, Jacobs has been 'doubly deauthorized' in her testimony (Jones 2002, 158).[22] Parramore's observation about the rigid enforcement of hierarchy in the South is correct, although it misses the point. Hierarchy is not simply a value held by that society but was a tool necessary for the maintenance of the slave system upon which Southern life was built. The rigorous and relentless effort spent preserving that hierarchy by the likes of Norcom serves that end. There is no reason, then, to assume that Norcom is acting from genuinely noble principles and virtuous motives, any more than a self-serving urge – though perhaps subconscious and internalised as a belief in his superiority – to protect his own reputation and standing at the top.

Rather than viewing Norcom and Jacobs through the filter of a hierarchical system that has been developed by the privileged parties, we must try to weigh the evidence fairly, part of which is to take Jacobs's testimony seriously. In emphasising the dignity, virtue, self-respect and agency of female slaves in particular, Jacobs tackles the first horn of the double deauthorisation. Whether or not Norcom would behave as Jacobs alleges is a more subjective question. But accepting her as a credible witness is the first step in approaching it. Beyond that, there is more than a suggestion of Norcom's domineering, factious and obsessive behaviour

---

[22] Jones prefigures the idea of epistemic injustice associated with Miranda Fricker. Fricker argues that epistemic justice is a necessary condition for republican freedom (2013). Using different language, I make a comparable case, drawing on Wollstonecraft (Coffee 2013, 2014).

in the evidence that Parramore himself offers, as well as from Yellin's extended investigations (2004). Furthermore, since the rampant sexual abuse of slaves by slaveholders is widely attested to, there can be no presumption against Norcom having committed it.[23]

5.2 Southern Propaganda

The first thing that Jacobs wrote for public consumption was her 'Letter from a Fugitive Slave' to the *New York Daily Tribune* in 1853 (§1.2). It was written as a reply to a letter written some six months earlier by Julia Gardiner Tyler, the wife of former president John Tyler. Tyler's letter was, in turn, written as a response to the Duchess of Sutherland's petition against American slavery, known at the Stafford House Address.[24] Although Tyler's letter was not actually published in the *Tribune*, her exchange with Sutherland had generated a fair amount of discussion amongst its readers, including a letter from Karl Marx.

Tyler's letter is very well written – highly polished, measured and diplomatic (if often cutting and sarcastic) in tone, and a masterclass in political spin, misdirection, and obfuscation. Indeed, its strident dismissal of any hint of criticism of the South carries an almost sinister tone. Tyler does not attempt to justify slavery. Instead, she deflects criticism by suggesting that it is politically motivated and self-serving. In so doing, Tyler's strategy may strike a chord with readers of today's political discourse as she shifts effortlessly between maintaining that 'we have done nothing wrong' to 'what Britain has done is far worse', and '*if* any wrong has been committed, it was by Britain, and we are the ones putting it right'. Though Tyler does not use the term 'fake news', her tactics are familiar: no one criticises Russian serfdom – and if they tried, 'the newspaper press would admonish you of the danger of interfering in that quarter' – so why are they criticising us? (Tyler 1853).

Although the Duchess of Sutherland acted in a personal capacity, representing neither the British government nor its people, Tyler reframes their exchange in nationalistic terms. It was Britain that pioneered the infamous transatlantic slave trade, amassing a monumental profit. Only after the British lost their monopoly in trafficking, following the Americans' victory

---

[23] In addition to Jacobs's testimony and Picquet's narrative, the diaries of Thomas Thistlewood (1721–1786) candidly record his rape and abuse of his female slaves (*Thomas Thistlewood Papers*, https://archives.yale.edu/repositories/11/resources/1050).

[24] As it happened, Jacobs and Sutherland would later meet during Jacobs's visit to England promoting her book in 1861. Greatly interested in her story, the Duchess invited Jacobs to stay at her house for some weeks (*Papers* 350–1).

against colonial oppression (a form of slavery), did they turn against the trade. Brazenly, Tyler suggests that it was the Americans themselves that 'abolished the slave trade' through their revolution.

As she proceeds, Tyler attempts to have things both ways. Although Britain was at fault in pioneering the transatlantic slave trade, the Americans have merely inherited the 'property' generated. 'The African, under her policy, and by her laws, became property. That property has descended from father to son, and constitutes a large part of Southern wealth. We desire no intrusion of advice as to our individual property rights'. Slavery has not been mentioned, only 'property', leaving aside its human character. Lest she be pressed on this point, Tyler turns the spotlight back on Britain: 'we meddle not with your laws of primogeniture and entail, although they are obnoxious to all our notions of justice and are in violation of the laws of nature'. In any case, the Americans deserve credit for repairing Britain's wrongs, she goes on. By repatriating freed negroes to newly 'independent States', they 'retribute the wrongs done by England to Africa by returning civilization for barbarism – Christianity for idolatry'.

The principal rhetorical line to which these arguments build is that Britain should stay out of American affairs. Slavery is what Tyler refers to as a 'domestic institution', and so the province of the Americans to handle themselves. 'We', she insists, 'prefer to work out our destiny alone'. It does not matter to Tyler that Sutherland is acting as an individual, Britain's track record on the matter of slavery is abysmal, and Britons should concentrate on addressing the condition of 'the poor, the stricken, the hungry and the naked of your own land', including the famine in Ireland. 'Women of England!' Tyler exhorts, 'go thither with your tender charities'.

It is on this point that Marx's intervention plays into Tyler's hands. In February 1853, shortly after Tyler's letter – although he does not mention it – Marx published his reply to Sutherland. He sidesteps the subject matter of 'Negro-Slavery', focussing entirely on the Duchess's admittedly highly troubling role in the Highland Clearances – a brutal and systematic process of eviction of the poor from agricultural land that was to be more profitably repurposed, with Marx noting that 15,000 Gaels, or crofters, were 'superseded by 131,000 sheep' (Marx 1853). As with much of what Tyler says about Britain's imperial and colonial atrocities, this is a legitimate point of criticism. But in a debate about the abolition of chattel slavery, Marx's approach only helps the Southerners' case, handing them an additional piece of 'whataboutism'. The conclusion to Marx's letter might almost have been written by Tyler herself: 'the enemy of

British Wage-Slavery has a right to condemn Negro-Slavery; a Duchess of Sutherland, ... a Manchester Cotton-lord—never!' (Marx 1853).

The most pertinent aspect of Tyler's letter for our purposes is the manner in which she frames it as a reply on behalf of the American – specifically Southern – woman, who is unable to reply for herself, so dutifully does she confine 'herself within that sphere for which the God who created her seems to have designed her' (Tyler 1853). Tyler presents an idyllic picture of Southern Christian womanhood, conjuring an image of 'that neatness and order, and that contentment, [which] is in nothing more observable than in the well clothed and happy domestics who welcome your arrival, and heap upon you every comfort during your sojourn under the roofs of their masters'. It is, Tyler argues, the province of Southern women 'to preside over the domestic economy of the estates and plantations of their husbands', including to 'attend to the comfort of all the labourers upon such estates'. It is, therefore, insulting to the dignity of Southern women to presume to intrude in their domain and 'introduce other superintendence other than their own'. To criticise a Southern women's management of her 'servants' would be akin to criticising how she raised her children. It is not only an insult to the women of the South, but it is an attempt to destroy the Union. Tyler, like so many Southern apologists, prefers to speak of 'labourers' or 'servants' rather than slaves, just as she spoke of 'domestic institutions' rather than of slavery. Indeed, she tends to reserve the term slavery either in an abstract sense or, more commonly, to condemn Britain's role in it.

Very briefly and peremptorily, Tyler denies the two specific charges raised against the slaveholders in the Stafford House Address – that slave families are callously separated (responding that this happens only rarely, and then in 'peculiar circumstances'), and that they are denied access to religious teaching. In *Incidents*, as we noted above (§§2.5, 3.6), Jacobs addresses the question of slaveholder religion. What moved her to write in response to Tyler, however, was the separation of families – 'I felt so indignant', she wrote to Amy Post (*Papers* 201). Her initial title for the letter was to be 'Slaves Sold Under Peculiar Circumstances', although this became the published subtitle.

If Tyler claims to represent white Southern women with no one to speak up for them, then Jacobs writes as a black woman, and in particular as 'a slave myself' (*Papers*, 197). In contrast to Tyler's slippery erudition, Jacobs employs a bluntly direct approach. She does not attempt to address the totality of Tyler's position but picks up on just one point – the treatment of families – that Tyler had slipped in almost in passing, and presses it home with a powerful and expansive personal testimony. Though she claims in the letter to lack both skill and education, she shows herself to be as tactically astute as her opponent, mobilising the emotive power of a first person narrative ('the truth', she observes, 'can never be told so well through the second and third person as from yourself', 198). Any subsequent lack of polish in Jacobs's letter then becomes a strength rather than a deficiency, adding authenticity to her words. In fact, although the situation she describes did reflect the general reality of plantation life, and was quite likely somebody's actual story, it was not, as she claimed in her (admittedly anonymous) letter, Jacobs's own.

The events and themes that Jacobs touches on in the letter are all subsequently developed extensively in *Incidents*, including the cruelty and Christian hypocrisy of the slaveholders. In her letter, however, although Tyler's remarks about not separating families motivated her to write, Jacobs uses this idea to introduce her principal theme, the sexual abuse of slaves by lecherous masters with absolute power. Her language is less veiled than in *Incidents*, referring to 'the indignities and vices imposed on [female slaves] by their lords of body and soul' (199). As the young victim reaches her twenties, 'she was less the object to be desired by the fiend who crushed her', and 'as her children grew, they bore too strong a resemblance to him who desired to give them no other inheritance save Chains'. Jacobs is also explicit about the 'strong rivalry between a handsome mulatto girl and a jealous and faded mistress'. For the mistress, she must content herself with her material wealth and trappings, but for the victim, she is 'sold by her seducer and master, caring not where, so that it puts him in possession of enough to purchase another victim' (200). In laying this explosive testimony bare, Jacobs cuts through the mannered obfuscation of Tyler's idealised Christian south, and establishes herself as a formidable opponent in the ideological war.

5.3 Lasting Division

It has been suggested that Tyler's letter was simply a pedestrian rehash of standard proslavery arguments and sentimental pastoralism (Yellin 2004, 122). This underestimates Tyler's political skill. The letter's use of standard tropes is a feature rather than a flaw. Tyler is aware of the value of creating and sustaining a powerful narrative. She refers to America's moral reputation, for example, as 'a power more resistless and more certain in its results – the power of example – the example of a free, prosperous, and great people, among whom all artificial distinctions of society are unknown, where preferment is equally open to all, and man's capacity for self-government is recognised' (1853). Tyler's letter should not be regarded as an isolated intervention. She wrote within what we might today call an ideological ecosystem in which proslavery newspapers, columnists, politicians, and civic and religious leaders all wrote in a mutually supportive manner to advance the Southern cause. Tyler's letter was political rather than philosophical, and so it was tactically effective for her to propagate the same message that was being consistently drummed out, shamelessly seizing the rhetorical high ground as artfully as any current partisan press secretary or spin doctor.

A notable feature of the Southern disinformation about slaveholding was the united front that was presented across the various parts of the movement. No dissent was brooked, just as we find today in authoritarian political movements. Jacobs recognises this in *Incidents*, writing, 'the northern man is not welcome south of Mason and Dixon's line, unless he suppresses every thought and feeling at variance with their "peculiar institution". Nor is it enough to be silent. The masters are not pleased, unless they obtain a greater degree of subservience than that; and they are generally accommodated' (*Incidents*, 42). Cutting through the ideological dogma, specious reasoning and political cant was very difficult for many people in the North far removed from the practices of slavery, some of whom would make the journey South to see the situation for themselves. Jacobs welcomes this but adds some cautionary advice: 'if you want to be fully convinced of the abominations of slavery, go on a southern plantation, and call yourself a negro trader. Then there will be no concealment; and you will see and hear things that will seem to you impossible among human beings with immortal souls' (48).

When Jacobs entered the abolition debate in 1853, she stepped into an ideological arena that has shaped America ever since. While this may seem like a platitude, the depth of feeling and division that remain, woven into the fabric of everyday life, was brought home to me on a recent visit to Edenton. Although there is a state historical marker recognising Jacobs's ties to the area on the main thoroughfare as one enters the town, by far the most prominent monument in Edenton is the memorial to 'Our Confederate Dead 1861–1865' bearing the initials CSA (Confederate States of America) a few hundred yards away at the end of the same street. The statue occupies the most prominent spot in town, on the waterfront overlooking the Chowan River. The contrast with Jacobs's sign is striking – I drove past that several times before I spotted it. You cannot miss the 8m high confederate memorial in the centre of town! The statue was erected at the turn of the twentieth century by the United Daughters of the Confederacy in the midst of an explicitly white supremacist political campaign in Edenton (Cecelski 2021). Relocated during the Civil Rights era to its current spot, the statue has become the focus of an intense and acrimonious struggle over its future in the wake of the Black Lives Matter protests of 2020, with calls for its removal as a racist symbol met by counter-allegations of erasing history. The town is split, and feelings run high.[25] More poignantly, the arguments and rhetoric of the nineteenth century are being repeated in our own time.

In this small town where Jacobs grew up, then, we can see something of the depth of divided and entrenched cultural feeling that is the inevitable legacy left by the institutionalised practice of slavery, even 160 years after its formal abolition.

5.4 No Easy Solutions

> My master had power and law on his side; I had a determined will. There is might in each (Incidents, 75).

These were Jacobs's words shortly before she first took flight. She captured an important aspect of the nature of slavery. Her battle was not with an individual, or even with a family or community of slaveholders, but with an institution. Slavery is not a bilateral relationship between individuals – enslaver and enslaved – but a practice built into the fabric of society. Slavery was backed up by the law and reinforced in the cultural norms and practices. On both counts, it was not just the slaveholders but the whole of society who were participants in slavery's wrongs.

An implication of this is that, while there was great power in Jacobs's resistance – she outwitted an intelligent, determined and well-connected opponent against seemingly insurmountable odds – there is only so much that individuals can do. Slavery is a structural form of domination, and the power of determined wills must come from a collective resistance. When Jacobs landed in Philadelphia, standing for the first time on supposedly 'free soil', her joy was tempered by the enormity of what she now faced: 'we had escaped from slavery, and we supposed ourselves to be safe from the hunters. But we were alone in the world, and we had left dear ties behind us' (133). And although Jacobs and her supporters had to act in the margins of society, outside of the law, their pursuers had the law's full backing ('while the Free States sustain a law which hurls fugitives back into slavery, how can the slaves resolve to become free men?', 40).

---

[25] See for example, https://spectrumlocalnews.com/nc/charlotte/news/2025/05/21/confederate-monument-memorial-debate-north-carolina.

A second implication is that there is no escaping slavery's moral corruption. Just as the British abolitionists who boycotted slave-produced goods such as sugar in the early nineteenth century could not avoid living in a nation that had grown rich from this trade, so no white Americans could entirely escape entanglement with an institution so integral to its national life.

So morally degraded had the nation become, that there were few easy answers to the ethical dilemmas that one might confront. Jacobs gives the example of a woman who inherited a female slave and her six children. One might think that she should simply have manumitted them. Indeed, she made just this offer to the enslaved family before she got married. They declined, knowing her to be a very good mistress. The woman's new husband soon showed his true colours, however: immediately, 'the new master claimed this family as his property' – a euphemism that strongly implies that he raped or abused the wife and those of her daughters who were of age (46). Given the marital laws and customs of the time, the mistress could no longer protect the family. The mother's boys were sold, and her girls were taken from her to the plantation, where two of them bore the master's children and another went insane from the abuse (the master's wife wept, knowing that 'her own husband had violated the purity she had so carefully inculcated'). The only child left was the little girl 'too young *to be of service*' to the master (my emphasis).

The story highlights several dilemmas facing the protagonists. Should the heiress have manumitted her slaves earlier, even against their will? Should the family have taken the opportunity for freedom? There is no suggestion that the mother was too shiftless to accept the responsibilities of independence. It simply may not have been a viable option for a black woman with a large family – and remember, having children was often not a choice even for married slave women – without the education or marketable skills to support herself in a harsh, racist society with few employment options and strict laws about vagrancy and burdening the state. Should the slave woman's free black husband have intervened to prevent the abuse? He tried his best and hid the children in the woods. This was a crime for which he was jailed and his sons sold. Should the slaveholder's wife have done more to protect her slaves? In a patriarchal society, she no longer had any say. Where the institutional practice of slavery exerts its grip, there simply is no easy solution. According to Jacobs, the slaveholder himself was not even a particularly cruel owner overall ('he was called a good master, for he fed and clothed his slaves better than most ... and the lash was not heard ... so frequently', 47). In another life, this man may possibly have seemed decent. 'Had it not been for slavery', Jacobs concludes, 'he would have been a better man, and his wife a happier woman'. One might say, there but for God's grace go any of us.

5.5 Racial Prejudice

> [My son] rattled away as fast as his tongue could do ... 'I'spose free boys can get along here at the north as well as white boys.' I did not like to tell the sanguine, happy little fellow how much he was mistaken (Incidents, 145).

Lest we think that only the South was at fault for slavery, Jacobs reminds us that both parts of the US worked together in lockstep – 'when victims make their escape from the wild beast of Slavery, northerners consent to act the part of bloodhounds, and hunt the poor fugitive back into his den' (34, also 41, 157). In one respect, however, the North matched and may even have surpassed the South – racial prejudice.

'Every where', Jacobs tells us, she 'found the same manifestations of that cruel prejudice, which so discourages the feelings, and represses the energies of the colored people' (146, her spelling). One of the most visible reminders of black people's social subordination was the public segregation they encountered. Jacobs was, for example, consigned to Jim Crow cars, kept below deck on the steamers, and made to eat in the kitchen rather than dining room in hotels. Even the intervention of white allies, such as Mary Stace Willis, had only a limited effect against the tide of visible public resentment at Jacobs's presence, and did little to diminish her sense of alienation. 'I found it hard to preserve my self-control', she recalls, 'when I looked round, and saw women who were nurses, as I was, and only one shade lighter in complexion, eyeing me with a defiant look, as if my presence were a contamination' (147). This was one occasion where Jacobs stood up for herself and won, telling the hotel landlord that 'there was no difference in the price of board for colored and white servants, and there was no justification for difference of treatment'. She also spoke out against the other black nannies for 'not having too much self-respect to submit to such treatment'.

Jacobs's disdainful comments towards others who failed to stand up for themselves was understandable, though I believe it should be taken in the same spirit as her remarks in §4.2 about 'willing slaves' – more as defiant self-assertion than as a considered moral judgement on those too browbeaten to resist. She concludes this anecdote, and the chapter on northern prejudice, with a powerful rallying call – 'let every colored man and woman do this, and eventually we shall cease to be trampled under foot by our oppressors' (147). In one sense, she is right. Where oppression is systematic and embedded in the social and cultural fabric, resistance is only effective when it is a collective effort. At the same time, taken on its own, the injunction underplays both the complexity of racism's deep cultural and institutional roots and the vicious intensity of the resistance that black Americans would face – right up to the present day. Structural racism has proven more resilient even than slavery.

5.6 A Qualified Freedom

> Reader, my story ends with freedom; not in the usual way, with marriage. I and my children are now free! (Incidents, 166).

These words come in the penultimate paragraph of Jacobs's book. The uplifting note is, however, immediately qualified. Her family is 'as free from the power of the slaveholders as are the white people of the north', which she notes, 'is not saying a great deal'. Her dream of a home with a hearthstone and her family around her has not been realised, nor would it ever be. She knows that she has come a long way from where she started, for which she is grateful. All the same, she is only partially free. After all, following the Dred Scott decision – whose words she subverted (§2.5) – she was not even a US citizen. In the slaveholding South, the lines were clear between freeman and slave. But in the North – where the talk was of freedom and equality, but the reality was backlash, subversion, obfuscation and marginalisation – the battle for freedom has been much harder to fight. It remains with us today. If this seems unjust, Jacobs was all too aware of that. 'Surely there must be some justice in man', she wondered, before remembering 'with a sigh, how slavery perverted all the natural feelings of the human heart' (120).

6 Final Reflections

> Some people are mere nonentities, or, are merely negative quantities. They leave no very clear or marked impression upon those with whom they are associated. It was not so however, in her case .... She rose above the dead level of mediocrity, like the mountain peaks that shoot above the mountain range (Francis Grimké, Papers, 828, Smyth 1985).

The quotation above comes from Francis Grimké's eulogy for Jacobs after her death in 1897. It is a touching and personal tribute that stands in contrast to the formal obituary from the *Boston Herald* that follows it in the collection of Jacobs's family papers (831–3). The obituary simply describes her as a slave who escaped who then went on to write 'a touching little story of her life', invoking an image of a plucky 'mulatto' with a harrowing tale who survives through the support of white well-wishers (831). Indeed, although Jacobs's time in the garret was not mentioned, her meeting the Duchess of Sutherland was singled out; the implication being, presumably, that it would have been a highlight in the life of a humble slave to have risen to having been entertained by the aristocracy. Grimké's eulogy, by contrast, deliberately avoids recounting Jacobs's life story. Instead, he gives the congregants an insight into her mind, character, personality, charisma and faith – in short, he presents Jacobs as a human being with an inner life.

The eulogy is poignant for our purposes, since one of the great achievements of *Incidents* is that it gives an account of slavery from the inside, not just from within the institution but within the mind of the human being who finds herself enslaved. The slave is not just theorised about but listened to, and in listening we the readers are not preached to but engaged with. Jacobs brings out the humanity in the people she talks about. The dehumanised slave is not an abstract concept but a rounded character who thinks, loves, fears, has hopes and makes plans, even against all odds. Harriet and John could have been any one of us growing up. By scratching beneath the surface of the cunning, obsequious or loyal slave, we find a rational agent with a plan. It is not only the slaves themselves that are humanised, but the slaveholders too. For all the enormity of what they did as purveyors of human flesh, Jacobs shows them not as monsters but as weak and conflicted human beings, and as part of a social system – albeit one which many of them worked hard to create and maintain – from which there was no simple way out. We also see behind the curtain of the relationships between slaves. In all this, Jacobs has gone far beyond what any other writer about slavery that I am aware of has managed to achieve.[26]

Jacobs does not simply portray slave life; she also analyses the nature of slavery philosophically, bringing her rich understanding of what it is to be a freedom-loving human being under the most terrifying and absolute form of domination – that of being the literal property and plaything

---

[26] This is, perhaps, an extravagant claim and is not meant to diminish other first person accounts of slavery such as those by Frederick Douglass, Olaudah Equiano, Elizabeth Keckley, Mary Prince, Sojourner Truth, Samuel Ringgold Ward, or later analyses such as those by W. E. B. Du Bois or Anna Julia Cooper. My comment is not about overall value but about Jacobs's unique blend of psychological insight, authenticity, and philosophical acuity.

of another in a society that approves of this happening – to her broader political analysis and social criticism. I have presented that analysis from a republican standpoint, though I welcome the fact that other scholars approach her from different perspectives. Jacobs certainly has a great deal to offer contemporary republican theorists. Perhaps her most important contribution starts with her exposure of the routine, omnipresent and extreme sexual abuse of female slaves that creates an environment where no woman can ever feel herself free from either the predatory eyes of men slaveholders or the potentially judgemental eyes of everybody else. Integrating this into the republican model, Jacobs lays the foundation for a feminist republicanism. She also articulates a relational form of independence in which freedom is a good that must be shared by those one is connected to. For all her personal bravery and genius, she was not a self-made woman but someone who relied on the support of others, cultivated strong relationships herself, and who prioritised the good of those she loved over her own well-being. Beyond her feminist republicanism, her work contributes to fields such as relational autonomy, structural domination and epistemic injustice.

On a personal note, I can say that immersing myself in Jacobs's life and philosophy has been by far the most-rewarding and eye-opening project that I have yet undertaken. Grimké's words at the start of this section could apply as much to Jacobs's philosophy as to her personality. Every reader knows just how much philosophy is mediocre, but like the tallest peak that shoots above the mountain range, *Incidents* rises above the dead level. It stands as an original, insightful and humane book that is shocking and provocative, but always enlightening.

Cast of Characters

Incidents was published anonymously with fictionalised names. I refer to the book's major characters by their real names as follows:

1. *Jacobs Family*

Historical	Pseudonym	Relationship/Role
Harriet Jacobs	Linda Brent	Author, Protagonist
John Swanson Jacobs	William Brent	Brother
Molly Horniblow	Aunt Martha	Grandmother
Delilah Horniblow	Mother	Mother (Molly's daughter)
Elijah Knox	Father	Father
Joseph Horniblow	Uncle Benjamin	Uncle (Molly's son)
Mark Ramsey	Uncle Phillip	Uncle (Molly's son)
Betty Horniblow	Aunt Nancy	Aunt (Delilah's twin)
Joseph Jacobs	Benny	Son (by Sawyer)
Louisa Matilda Jacobs	Ellen	Daughter (by Sawyer)

2. *Horniblow-Norcom Family*

Historical	Pseudonym	Relationship/Role
Elizabeth Pritchard Horniblow	Martha's mistress	Molly's mistress (Hannah's sister)
Hannah Pritchard	Miss Fanny	Elizabeth's sister
Margaret Horniblow	Kind mistress	Elizabeth's daughter (Mary Matilda's sister)
Mary Matilda Horniblow Norcom	Mrs Flint	Elizabeth's daughter (James Norcom's wife)
James Norcom	Dr Flint	Main antagonist
Mary Matilda Norcom Messmore	Miss Emily	Norcoms' daughter (Harriet's legal owner)

3. *Others*

Historical	Pseudonym	Relationship/Role
Samuel Tredwell Sawyer	Mr Sands	Father of Harriet's children
Mary Blount Tredwell	Mrs Hobbs	Sawyer's cousin
Martha Hoskins Rombough Blount	Kind lady	Harboured Harriet in Edenton

(Continued)

Historical	Pseudonym	Relationship/Role
Nathaniel Parker Willis	Mr Bruce	Harriet's employer
Mary Stace Willis	Mrs Bruce (first)	Harriet's employer/friend
Cornelia Grinnell Willis	Mrs Bruce (second)	Harriet's employer/friend

Abbreviations

Bondage   Frederick Douglass, *My Bondage and My Freedom*. London: Penguin (2003 [1855]).

Despots   John Swanson Jacobs, *The United States Governed by Six Hundred Thousand Despots: A True Story of Slavery*. Edited by Jonathan Schroeder, Chicago: University of Chicago Press (2024 [1855]).

Incidents   Harriet Jacobs, *Incidents in the Life of a Slave Girl*. Second Norton Critical Edition. Edited by Frances Smith Foster and Richard Yarborough. New York: W. W. Norton (2019 [1861]).

Papers   *The Harriet Jacobs Family Papers*. Edited by Jean Fagan Yellin, Chapel Hill: University of North Carolina Press (2008).

References

Bailyn, Bernard. (1992). *The Ideological Origins of the American Revolution*. Cambridge, MA: Belknap Press.

Bergès, Sandrine and Alan Coffee (eds). (Forthcoming). "Recognising Women's Contribution to the History of Republican Theorising." In *Women and Republicanism*. Oxford: Oxford University Press.

Blassingame, John. (1972). *The Slave Community: Plantation Life in the American South*. Oxford: Oxford University Press, 480–85.

Boxill, Bernard. (2018). "The Fight with Covey." In *A Political Companion to Frederick Douglass*, edited by Neil Roberts. Lexington: University Press of Kentucky, 61–83.

Braxton, Joanne. (1986). "Harriet Jacobs' *Incidents in the Life of a Slave Girl*: The Redefinition of the Slave Narrative Genre." *Massachusetts Review*. 27 (2): 379–87.

Bromell, Nick. (2013). *The Time Is Always Now: Black Thought and the Transformation of US Democracy*. Oxford: Oxford University Press.

Bromell, Nick. (2021). "Harriet Jacobs: Prisoner of Hope." In *African American Political Thought: A Collected History*, edited by Melvin Rogers and Jack Turner. Chicago: University of Chicago Press, 101–22.

Cecelski, David. (2021). "Edenton and the Battle for White Supremacy." https://davidcecelski.com/2021/05/07/edenton-and-the-battle-for-white-supremacy/

Coffee, Alan. (2013). "Mary Wollstonecraft, Freedom and the Enduring Power of Social Domination." *European Journal of Political Theory*. 12 (2): 116–35.

Coffee, Alan. (2014). "Two Spheres of Domination: Republican Theory, Social Norms and the Insufficiency of Negative Freedom." *Contemporary Political Theory*. 14 (1): 45–62.

Coffee, Alan. (2019). "Women and the History of Republicanism". *Australasian Philosophical Review*. 4 (1): 361–9.

Coffee, Alan. (2020). "A Radical Revolution in Thought: Frederick Douglass on the Slave's Perspective on Republican Freedom". In *Radical Republicanism: Recovering the Tradition's Popular Heritage*, edited by Bruno Leipold, Karma Nabulsi and Stuart White. Oxford: Oxford University Press, 47–64.

Coffee, Alan. (2023). "Mary Wollstonecraft and Wollstonecraftian Philosophy." In *The Oxford Handbook of American and British Women*

Philosophers in the Nineteenth Century, edited by Lydia Moland and Alison Stone. Oxford: Oxford University Press, 46–61.

Coffee, Alan. (2024). "Interpersonal and Structural Domination: Frederick Douglass and the Invisible Chains that Bind Us." *Social Theory and Practice*. 50 (4): 543–565.

Coffee, Alan. (2025). *Mary Wollstonecraft: Independent Woman*. London: Polity.

Coffee, Alan. (Forthcoming). "The Radical Nature of Women's Republicanism." In *Radical Republicanism in Early Modern Europe*, edited by Anna Becker, Nicolai von Eggers Mariegaard, and Alessandro Mulieri. Leiden: Brill.

Douglass, Frederick. (1881). "The Color Line." *The North American Review*. CXXXII: 567–77.

Douglass, Frederick. (1976). *The Life and Writings of Frederick Douglass*. Edited by Philip Foner, 5 volumes. New York: International Publishers.

Douglass, Frederick. (1979). *The Frederick Douglass Papers*. Edited by John Blassingame and John McKivigan, Series 1, 5 volumes. New Haven, CT: Yale University Press.

Douglass, Frederick. (2002). *My Bondage and My Freedom*. London: Penguin.

Ernest, John. (2014). *The Oxford Handbook of the African American Slave Narrative*. Oxford: Oxford University Press.

Fricker, Miranda. (2013). "Epistemic justice as a condition of political freedom?" *Synthese*. 190: 1317–1332.

Furstenberg, Francois. (2003). "Beyond freedom and slavery: Autonomy, virtue, and resistance in early American political discourse." *Journal of American History*. 89 (4): 1295–1330.

Gaius. (1904). *Gai Institutiones or Institutes of Roman Law by Gaius*. Edited by Edward Poste. Oxford: Clarendon Press.

Garfield, Deborah and Rafia Zafar (eds). (1996). *Harriet Jacobs and Incidents: New Critical Essays*. Cambridge: Cambridge University Press.

Gass, Conard. (2022). "Norcom, James, Sr." NCpedia. Dictionary of North Carolina Biography. University of North Carolina Press. Accessed on March 8, 2025. www.ncpedia.org/biography/norcom-james-sr.

Gooding-Williams, Robert. (2011). *In the Shadow of Du Bois: Afro-Modern Political Thought in America*. Cambridge: Harvard University Press.

Gourevitch, Alex. (2015). *From Slavery to the Cooperative Commonwealth: Labor and Republican Liberty in the Nineteenth Century*. Cambridge: Cambridge University Press.

References

Green, Karen. (2019). "On the philosophical significance of eighteenth-century 'Republicans'". *Australasian Philosophical Review*. 3 (4): 371–80.

Hartman, Saidiya. (1997). *Scenes of Subjection*. London: Norton.

Jacobs, John. (2024). *The United States Governed by Six Hundred Thousand Despots: A True Story of Slavery*. Edited by Jonathan Schroeder. Chicago: University of Chicago Press.

Jacobs, Harriet. (2008). *The Harriet Jacobs Family Papers*. Edited by Jean Yellin, Joseph Thomas, Kate Culkin, and Scott Korb. Chapel Hill: University of North Carolina Press.

Jacobs, Harriet. (2019). *Incidents in the Life of a Slave Girl*. Second Norton Critical Edition. Edited by Frances Smith Foster and Richard Yarborough. New York: W. W. Norton.

Jagmohan, Desmond. (2022). "Peculiar Property: Harriet Jacobs on the Nature of Slavery." *Journal of Politics*. 84 (2): 669–681.

Jones, Karen. (2002). "The Politics of Credibility." In *A Mind of One's Own: Feminist Essays on Reason and Objectivity*, edited by Louise Antony and Charlotte Witt. Boulder, CO: Westview Press, 152–76.

Kirkland, Frank. (2015). "Is an Existential Reading of the Fight with Covey Sufficient to Explain Frederick Douglass's Critique of Slavery?." *Critical Philosophy of Race*. 3 (1): 124–51.

Kohn, Margaret. (2005). "Frederick Douglass's Master-Slave Dialectic." *The Journal of Politics*. 67 (2): 497–514.

Long, John Wesley. (1917). *Early History of the North Carolina Medical Society*. North Carolina: s.n.

Marx, Karl. (1853). "The Duchess of Sutherland and Slavery." New York Daily Tribune, February 9.

Milton, John. (1991). *Political Writings*. Edited by Martin Dzelzainis. Cambridge: Cambridge University Press.

Parramore, Thomas. (1990). "Harriet Jacobs, James Norcom, and the Defense of Hierarchy." *Carolina Comments*. XXXVIII (3): 82–9.

Pettit, Philip. (1997). *Republicanism: A Theory of Freedom and Government*. Oxford: Oxford University Press.

Picquet, Louisa and Hiram Mattison. (1861). *Louisa Picquet, the Octoroon, or, Inside Views of Southern Domestic Life*. New York: The Author.

Price, Richard. (1991). *Political Writings*. Edited by D. O. Thomas. Cambridge: Cambridge University Press.

Rogers, Melvin. (2023). *The Darkened Light of Faith*. Princeton: Princeton University Press.

Skinner, Quentin. (2025). *Liberty as Independence: The Making and Unmaking of a Political Ideal*. Cambridge: Cambridge University Press.

Smyth, William. (1985). "O Death, where is Thy Sting?: Reverend Francis J. Grimké's Eulogy for Harriet A. Jacobs." *Journal of Negro History*. 70 (1/2): 35–9.

Spillers, Hortense. (1987). "Mama's Baby, Papa's Maybe: An American Grammar Book." *Diacritics*. 17 (2): 64–81.

Tyler, Julia Gardiner. (1853). "To the Duchess of Sutherland and the Ladies of England." New York Herald, January 28.

United States Bureau of Labor Statistics. (1934). *History of wages in the United States from colonial times to 1928* (Bulletin No. 604). U.S. Government Printing Office. https://fraser.stlouisfed.org/title/4054

Wollstonecraft, Mary. (1992), *A Vindication of the Rights of Woman*. London: Penguin.

Yellin, Jean. (1981). "Written by Herself: Harriet Jacobs' Slave Narrative." *American Literature*. 53 (3): 479–86.

Yellin, Jean. (2004). *Harriet Jacobs: A Life*. New York: Basic Civitas Books.

Acknowledgements

This Element was made possible by a Franklin Research Grant from the American Philosophical Society. I also thank Jacqui Broad for asking me to write on Jacobs and for her great patience with me during a difficult period of life.

Cambridge Elements =

Women in the History of Philosophy

Jacqueline Broad
Monash University

Jacqueline Broad is Professor of Philosophy at Monash University, Australia. Her area of expertise is early modern philosophy, with a special focus on seventeenth and eighteenth-century women philosophers. She is the author of *Women Philosophers of the Seventeenth Century* (Cambridge University Press, 2002), *A History of Women's Political Thought in Europe, 1400–1700* (with Karen Green; Cambridge University Press, 2009), and *The Philosophy of Mary Astell: An Early Modern Theory of Virtue* (Oxford University Press, 2015).

Advisory Board

Dirk Baltzly, *University of Tasmania*
Sandrine Bergès, *Bilkent University*
Marguerite Deslauriers, *McGill University*
Karen Green, *University of Melbourne*
Lisa Shapiro, *McGill University*
Emily Thomas, *Durham University*

About the Series

In this Cambridge Elements series, distinguished authors provide concise and structured introductions to a comprehensive range of prominent and lesser-known figures in the history of women's philosophical endeavour, from ancient times to the present day.

Cambridge Elements

Women in the History of Philosophy

Elements in the Series

Mary Wollstonecraft
Martina Reuter

Susan Stebbing
Frederique Janssen-Lauret

Harriet Taylor Mill
Helen McCabe

Victoria Welby
Emily Thomas

Nísia Floresta
Nastassja Pugliese

Catharine Trotter Cockburn
Ruth Boeker

Lucrezia Marinella
Marguerite Deslauriers

Amalia Holst
Andrew Cooper

Iris Murdoch
Bridget Clarke

Platonist Women
Crystal Addey

E. E. Constance Jones
Gary Ostertag

Harriet Jacobs
Alan. M. S. J. Coffee

A full series listing is available at: www.cambridge.org/EWHP

Printed by Integrated Books International,
United States of America